Become
God's Messenger

Daily Devotions from the book of Malachi

56 Passages for Prayerful Reading

by

Israel Harel

All Scripture unless otherwise mentioned are taken from the New King James Version®. Copyright © 1982 by Thomas Nelson. All rights reserved.

© Israel Harel 2016

Becoming God's Messenger

First and foremost, I want to thank God for the stroke I had few years back. Through that, God has taught me that He does not need me. He loves me and wants to use me, but He manages very well without me.
I also want to thank my wife and family that help me keep my life in balance.
Many thanks to all the people that made this book possible. Maya R. for the editing of the Hebrew, Michael Nessim for the help he was in the translation into English, for Hanna K. and Daniel G. for helping with the English proofreading and all the people that encouraged me through the preparation of this book. A big thank you!!!
Israel Harel
2thejews@gmail.com

Introduction

A father's last wishes expressed to his loved ones before his departure, or before his death are considered to be very important. A father who knows that he is leaving thinks of the most important message that he can leave behind for his loved ones. We see this in the Song of Moses and in his blessing (Deut. 31:14-33:29), in King David's last words to Solomon before his death (1 Ki. 2:1-10), and of course in Jesus' great commission. The people to whom the commissions and blessings were given received them very solemnly and were careful to carry them out.

Jesus' last commandment appears in Matthew 28:18-20: *And Jesus came and spoke to them, saying: "All authority has been given to Me in heaven and on earth. Go therefore and make disciples of all the nations, baptizing them in the name of the Father and of the Son and of the Holy Spirit, teaching them to observe all things that I have commanded you; and lo, I am with you always, even to the end of the age."* This commandment was not only given to believers during Jesus' time but to each one of us. Jesus is calling us to get up and go, to get out of our comfort zone and go to all those who don't believe in Him. We are called to go to them with a clear purpose: to make them disciples of Jesus. Jesus is calling each one of us to be his messenger. This book is a tool that is intended to help everyone who is interested in becoming a better messenger of God, and who wants to understand the essence of the message and the mission that God has given us.

This book is not an exegetical commentary trying to understand the writer's intention at the time of writing. It is a practical commentary that endeavors to understand how things the prophet wrote about back then apply to us today. It is a book that reflects on the words of Malachi, attempting to understand what we can learn from the writings of Malachi today. It is intended for prayerful reading therefore, after the introduction it is divided into short sections intended for daily devotional reading.

Malachi, which means "my messenger" in Hebrew, teaches us about the essence of being God's messenger, His requirements and what the message is. God's will has always been for *all the LORD's people to be prophets* (Num. 11:29). This means that all whom He has made His *kingdom of priests* (Ex 19:6, 1 Pet 2:9) have to be His messengers to *proclaim the praises of Him who called you out of darkness into His marvelous light* (1 Pet 2:9). This is also the purpose of the book of Malachi, the messenger. Every person claiming to be the *LORD's messenger, [speaking] the LORD's message to the people* (Haggai 1:13), has to deliver a clear message from the Lord. This message makes the hearers and recipients become message-bearers themselves, continuing the commission and passing on the message from the Lord. The messenger comes with a message that turns the hearers and recipients of the message into messengers themselves, who carry the message further - and so on and on.

The apostle Paul who responded to Jesus' command: *Go therefore and make disciples of all the nations* (Matt 28:19-20) (a command which was given to us all), became one of the most successful messengers ever. Paul helps us to understand the essence of the mission and of the messenger in the epistle to Titus 1:1-4a:

Paul, a bondservant (the actual word DULOS means a slave) *of God and an apostle* (a messenger, one that was sent) *of Jesus Christ, according to the faith of God's elect and the acknowledgment of the truth which accords with godliness, in hope of eternal life which God, who cannot lie, promised before time began, but has in due time manifested His word through preaching, which was committed to me according to the commandment of God our Savior; to Titus, a true son in our common faith.*

Paul understood that he was a slave of the Lord, which means he had a mission; he was commissioned to pass on a message. The bearing of the message was entrusted into his hands to pass on to Titus and to all of God's elect. The purpose of the message is not to exalt the messenger nor to make him famous, but to edify and build-up the hearers, *according to the faith of God's elect and the acknowledgment of the truth*. This mission delivered in godliness, and with the hope of eternal life is for the building of faith for those whom God has chosen. The purpose is that the hearers, God's elect, will know the truth and will themselves become God's messengers who in godliness and continual hope of eternal life will carry out God's mission by proclaiming His Word.

Who was Malachi and when was the book written?

There is no identifying detail about who Malachi is in the book of Malachi. We are not told who his father is, or who his mother is. We don't know where he came from and we can only suppose where he prophesied.

We conclude that he prophesied at the time when the temple was still standing and functioning, because he speaks to the priests engaged in the Lord's daily temple service. We understand he was active during the Persian rule since he speaks of the *"Pecha"* (English "governor") in 1:8, *"And when you offer the blind as a sacrifice, is it not evil? And when you offer the lame and sick, is it not evil? Offer it then to your governor!* [heb. *"Pecha"*] *Would he be pleased with you? Would he accept you favorably?"* says the LORD of hosts. *"Pecha"* is a ruler of a city or part of the country. Indeed, there were *"Pecha"*s also during Babylonian times, but at that time the temple was in ruins and therefore we understand that he prophesied during the time of the Persians.

He was most probably active at the time of Ezra and Nehemiah, 430-410 BC when all the conditions were met, i.e. there was a *"Pecha"* and a functioning temple where the priests served in the Holy Place.

All the prophetic books declare the name of the prophet in the first passage of the book. The book of Malachi starts with *'The burden of the word of the LORD to Israel by Malachi'*. However, we are not sure that his name was indeed Malachi, or merely a description of his role, as the meaning of Malachi in Hebrew is "My Messenger". The name Malachi does not appear anywhere else in the Scriptures nor in any external writing from that same period, unless it is speaking of Malachi the prophet. There were many assumptions in the Jewish writings as to who Malachi was. Most of them thought that Malachi was not his real name, although they did not know exactly who he was. According to one of the traditions it was Ezra the scribe, according to another it was Mordechai the Jew or Zerubbabel son of Shealtiel, etc.

In the Megillah tractate (a tractate of the Talmud) which was written a few hundred years after Malachi, we read some of the assumptions: 'Malachi is the same as Mordecai. Why was he called Malachi? Because he was next to the king'. They objected: 'Baruch the son of Neriah and Mordecai.' Haggai, Zechariah and Malachi all prophesied in the second year of Darius?! R. Joshua b. Korha said: 'Malachi is Ezra, and the Sages say that Malachi was his proper name.'*

Tradition claims here that he prophesied during the second year of Darius, but we know that the prophet prophesied when the temple already existed and was fully functioning. In several places mentioned in Ezra, during the second year of Darius the temple was not yet functioning, and its building work was only restated during that year (Ezra 4:24).

The Uniqueness of Malachi and Obadiah

Malachi together with Obadiah, is one of the two mysterious writers in the Old Covenant. For all other prophets we have identifying details of who they were or details regarding when and where they prophesied, or both. *The word of the LORD that came to Micah of Moresheth in the days of Jotham, Ahaz, and Hezekiah, kings of Judah, which he saw concerning Samaria and Jerusalem* (Micah 1:1) serves as a good example. Micah was a Morashtite, meaning he came from a place called Moresheth Gath, better known today as Maresha which is next to Beit Govrin in the area where I grew up. Micah prophesied in the days of Jotham, Ahaz and Hezekiah kings of Judah. The period in which he prophesied is specified in the book. Some of the books of the prophets contain fewer details about the prophet and his time. *Now the word of the LORD came to Jonah the son of Amittai, saying ...* (Jonah 1:1), this does not tell us during which period Jonah

---

* Mishnah, Megillah tractate 15a, 71
http://www.sefaria.org/Megillah.15a?lang=en&layout=block&sidebarLang=all

prophesied nor where he came from, but it does tell us who his father was and in so doing identifies him precisely. Habakkuk's identification is less clear. We do not know his place of birth or his father's name but we do get his identification as *'the prophet'* (*Habakkuk the prophet).* That is how he was known, and the use of the title *'the prophet'* identifies Habakkuk to the hearers. In contrast both Malachi and Obadiah do not bear any titles, and no identifying details are given about them about the period in which they prophesied nor about the place where they prophesied. We can draw some conclusions regarding the period in which they prophesied from the content of their prophecies, but there are no accurate descriptions. Even their names do not necessarily identify them, considering that Obadiah means "The Slave of the LORD" and Malachi means "My Messenger". It certainly seems as if these were not their real names but rather a description of their function.

In my opinion, one of the reasons for maintaining obscurity is that their message was a direct message from God through His messengers. God's Messengers, the prophets removed themselves from the message so as not to be an obstruction in conveying the message. Their message is not limited to time or place but is relevant to all generations and throughout the entire world. I am not saying that the messages of the other prophets are not relevant to all generations and in all places, to the contrary. However, it is easier to say regarding messages delivered in Jerusalem at Hezekiah's time for instance, that they were relevant then and do not speak directly to us today. Clearly the message of these prophets is a global message relevant to all periods, including ours.

The target audience of these two prophets are different. Obadiah speaks to Edom a hostile nation neighboring Israel. He warns them not to harm Israel when Israel is being judged, and not to partner with the nations that God is using to judge Israel in their attack on Israel. This message is appropriate for any time in human history and especially in these days when the nations are gathering against Jerusalem.

Malachi on the other hand, speaks to the priests, the Levites and Israel. His message is a clear and valid message for all times, for all those who are *a royal priesthood, a holy nation* (1 Pet. 2:9-10, quoting Exodus 19:6). It is actually a book of instruction to anyone who is sent by the Lord, who is His messenger. In this instruction book you find the job description, the message, the obstacles and the responses to the message and the messenger.

What is more important, the messenger or the mission?

As we have said, we do not know if Malachi was the name or the description of the prophet's role because Malachi means, "My Messenger". In my opinion it is his role, his calling. The reason the writer stated only his role, and not his name, is that he wanted to remove himself from the message. He wanted to be an efficient human messenger to convey the Sender's message perfectly. Therefore, he does not reveal his own identity, endeavoring not to mix his own character and voice with God's message.

The identity of the prophet at the time of his prophecy is not important to the prophet. He does not seek to put himself forward. His mission is more important to him than receiving recognition for being God's messenger. Likewise, it should be so for everyone who is sent by God. The messenger and the time is not important. The message is important during its time and beyond its time. The very fact that the messenger disappears, and all that remains is the message, is an important message in itself for all who strive to be God's messengers throughout history.

The goal of a good messenger is to effectively pass on the sender's message. Every prophet, every messenger of God conveyed God's message to the people he was sent to, but always mixed his own character and voice into the message in the process. In 1 Cor. 14:32, it is written that *'the spirits of prophets are subject to prophets.'* We know that Jeremiah was the crying prophet because his character was mixed with the message. Isaiah had a different character, as did Ezekiel and Zechariah. The message in the book of Malachi is God's direct message to the priests, Levites and the rest of the people. The prophet himself serves as an instrument, an emissary, as a messenger, but does not mix his character into the message. He manages to remove himself from the message in order to be a clear channel to convey a sharp and clear message to the people.

The book of Malachi is certainly an instruction manual for the messenger who desires to pass on his Sender's message in the clearest way. It contains both the requirements for the messenger, and the message that the messenger needs to deliver. In actual fact the messenger himself IS the message, and therefore it is important to God how the message is passed on and who the messenger is. God corrects, sanctifies and purifies the messenger so that the messenger himself will be a clear message of God's love. The aspiration for anyone who is sent by God has to be, as we see in the "Instruction Book", the book of Malachi, passing on the message in the clearest possible way without staining it with his own personal faults. The desire of every messenger of God has to be to make himself invisible as the mediator between the message and the people who are supposed to hear that message.

This is in complete contrast to what the spiritual (as well as the political) leaders of our nation do. Our rabbis did and continue to insert themselves as a prism between the Word of God and the nation in order to have influence over what the people hear. Even until today we as a nation suffer from this and cannot read the Scriptures without asking the everlasting question - "What do the rabbis say about this?"

Our leaders did the exact opposite of what Malachi did. He tried to make himself invisible as the mediator of the Word of God, whereas they forcefully assert themselves as mediators. Malachi tried to influence the message as little as possible; our rabbis try to influence the message as much as possible. While Malachi tried not to be seen and known; the rabbis want us to know only them and follow them.

Unfortunately, we see the same trends in the church today where people follow charismatic and famous leaders who serve as mediators between God and their followers. Christians feel they have to be famous in order to be effective messengers, which is exactly the opposite of what Malachi did.

The question each one of us has to ask himself is, "What kind of messenger am I? Am I trying to remove myself from the message I was given or trying to intensify my presence in the message? Am I trying to convey a pure message or am I mixing myself into it?" One of the ways to know if a teacher, preacher, evangelist, prophet or anyone else speaking by God's commission is indeed sent by God, is to observe whether his efforts are to make himself invisible in giving the message or to promote himself.

What about you? What kind of messenger are you? My prayer is that this book will help everyone seeking to be a better messenger carrying a clearer message. As stated before, this book was written in order to be a helpful instrument to its readers. Every day when you read the Scriptures and pray, read at least one passage from this book as well. Consider prayerfully whether there is something in the passage through which the Spirit of God desires to speak to you. If so, commit it to God in prayer. If necessary, repent; If needs be, give Him thanks. Seek His strength and will, and above all – ask Him to make you a messenger who glorifies his Sender; so that He will make you *the Lord's messenger,* speaking *the Lord's message.*

This booklet is intended to encourage discussion between you and God and I pray that it will do so.

Day 1

The burden *of the word of the LORD to Israel by Malachi.* (Malachi 1:1)

The very first words in the book describe the type of message and what is required of the messenger. Prophecies that are described as burdens in the Bible are solemn and unpleasant prophecies that speak of judgment and calamity, and are usually directed at the Gentiles. For instance, the burden against Babylon, the burden against Moab, the burden against Egypt, the burden against Dumah (Isaiah 13:1; 15:1; 17:1; 19:1; 21:11) and many others.

The book of Malachi starts with the words: *"The burden of the word of the LORD".* When we continue reading we understand that this burden is not one of judgment but one of love.

The word *burden* (Hebrew, *Masah*), which is used to describe visions, addresses prophecies of calamity or means a heavy load that someone carries. The word of the Lord is a burden. God has a heavy burden which He carries. Later on he explains what this burden is, but here he says: I have a heavy load, which I place into the hands of my messenger. It is my messenger's duty to carry this burden. Whoever wishes to be a messenger of God has to take God's burden upon himself and pass it on to the hearers.

Jesus declared similar things when He called out, *"If anyone desires to come after Me, let him deny himself, and take up his cross, and follow Me"* (Mat 16:24). As is written here, there are requirements for whoever wants to follow Jesus, to represent the Messiah and be His messenger.

What is required of him?

1. **To deny himself.** He must desire God's will more than his own will. He must desire to be a faithful messenger who represents his Sender, and understand that God's message is more important than being the messenger. Many of us think God will not manage without us; that if *we* don't pass on God's message, there won't be anyone else to do it. As messengers of Jesus, as those who have been called to fulfill "the great commission" (*"Go therefore and make disciples of all the nations, baptizing them in the name of the Father and of the Son and of the Holy Spirit, teaching them to observe all things that I have commanded you"* Mat. 28:18-20), we must deny ourselves. We are not the important ones, He is and the burden He carries and the message He is trying to convey. We must decrease so that He can increase.

2. **Take up the cross of the Messiah**. The messenger will carry the burden of God together with Him, and like the Messiah he would do it publicly without shame. God does not need help, but He gives us the privilege of joining Him in carrying the burden. *"Come to Me, all you who labor and are heavy laden, and I will give you rest. Take My yoke*

upon you and learn from Me, for I am gentle and lowly in heart, and you will find rest for your souls. For My yoke is easy and My burden is light." (Matthew 11:28-30). God calls us to be His partners in carrying His burden.

3.   **Follow the Messiah.** Step by step he will make sure to stay close to the Messiah, for if he moves away from the Messiah, he won't know where the Messiah is going or how to follow Him. If he stays close to the Messiah, he will walk on the paths that the Messiah walked, and behave as the Messiah behaved.

The Messiah is looking for people who will respond to His call to go to all the nations, will take up His burden and follow Him. God is looking for a messenger that He can point to, and call him "Malachi", "My messenger".

Can God call you "Malachi?" Can He trust you with His message?

Day 2

*The burden of **the word of the LORD** to Israel by Malachi.* (Malachi 1:1).

When the Word of the Lord starts to illuminate our lives, it first shines a light on our guilt as sinners, then frees us so that we can be sent out.

The written Word of God, the Holy Scriptures, is a mirror that reflects our true face. The Word of God is given to us so that we can look at our true reflection with God's light. As is written, *"he who looks into the perfect law of liberty"* (James 1:25), we then see ourselves in that light. The first thing that happens when we see ourselves in the light of the Holy Scriptures; we are shocked and refuse to accept the truth about ourselves. "I can't possibly be like that", we tell ourselves, and refuse to accept our ugly face, our difficult character, the hatred bubbling in our hearts and the hard words that come out of our mouths. "It's not me", we claim, "that's more like others." "I am good and faithful, nice and pleasant." Slowly we come to admit that the one we see in the light of the Scriptures which the Holy Spirit shines, is me! Then the cry bursts out from our hearts, *"Who will deliver me from this body of death?"* (Romans 7:24). When the cry is real and comes out from a broken heart, the Holy Spirit who is within us answers Grace! *"I thank God—through Jesus Christ our Lord!"* (Romans 7:25). And then the cry turns into a song of praise, *"Oh, give thanks to the LORD, for He is good!*

... *For His merciful kindness (*Hebrew:*Chesed,* meaning Grace*) is great toward us."* (Psalm 106:1, 117:2).

But it does not end here. The revelation of God's grace in our lives causes us to go out into the streets of the city and the market places to cry out with a great voice, *"there is no other name under heaven given among men by which we must be saved"* (Acts 4:12).

The Messiah is called "The Word of God" (Logos). The Word of God who showed us who we are, and who took on flesh, died on the cross, rose again and saved us by His grace making us *"workers together with Him"* (2 Corinthians 6:1). He calls us to carry His yoke, to carry His burden and to learn from Him. Carrying His burden expresses itself in our lives in that, *"the love of Christ compels us"* (2 Corinthians 5:14) and we preach the gospel of salvation by God's grace without seeking honor for ourselves. For *"woe is me if I do not preach the gospel"* (1 Corinthians 9:16).

Are you willing to be a partner in His work? Are you willing to bear His burden and cry out aloud in the city square, *"Jesus the Messiah, the King of Israel – He is the One we have been looking for!"*?

Day 3

*The burden of **the word of the LORD to Israel** by Malachi* (Malachi 1:1).

When God speaks, He speaks directly to those who belong to Him. The Word of God is personal and direct and is aimed at all those who are willing to hear. Our problem is that we are not willing to hear (as was also the problem with the children of Israel).

"Is not My word like a fire?" says the LORD, "and like a hammer that breaks the rock in pieces?" (Jeremiah 23:29) and *"For the word of God is living and powerful, and sharper than any two-edged sword, piercing even to the division of soul and spirit, and of joints and marrow, and is a discerner of the thoughts and intents of the heart."* (Hebrews 4:12). The breaking of the rock frightens us, especially when that rock is our heart.

It scares us to allow the Word of God to reveal what is really in our hearts, so we take measures to guard those corners that we want to be kept away from the Word of God. We hide them in the shade, in the dark, in *"the clefts of the rocks, and into the crags of the rugged rocks, from the terror of the LORD and the glory of His majesty."* (Isaiah 2:21), so that we don't see them. "Everyone does that" we excuse ourselves; "it is acceptable today"; "I am not hurting anyone"; "things are different these days". This we pronounce as we allow our eyes to wander to strange places, or our relationships with the other sex to develop further than is permitted in the Word of God. Saying to ourselves: "God does not really love us if He withholds from us what the flesh and the heart demands." By doing so we sound more like the serpent in the Garden of Eden. *God has said, "You shall not eat it lest you die." ... the serpent said to the woman, "You will not surely die!"* (Genesis 3:3-4).

First of all, the Word of God speaks to us personally in order to liberate and purify us. He wants to shatter the rock of our hearts, so that we can come closer to Him.
God is love. His burden, His desire, the thing He longs for and for which He sent Jesus the Messiah to taste death for us, is to bring us into an intimate relationship with Him. That is why He shines His light and removes anything that prevents this.

Are you willing to trust God that His thoughts toward you are for peace and not for evil, and to open the hidden corners of your heart before Him? Are you willing for God to shatter the rock of your heart, even if it hurts, so that you can be closer to Him? Are you ready to let the Word of God speak directly to you and shed light on the sins of your heart?

Day 4

The burden of the word of the LORD to Israel by Malachi. **"I have loved you," says the LORD** (Malachi 1:1-2).

The central declaration of God is His love, this He declares with a loud voice; a declaration which is the motive behind all of His doings, the declaration that is the essence of the burden that He carries, both at the cross and today.

This love drove Him to create the world, this love leads Him to plan us before He created the world, this love He showed us at the cross, and this love He shares with us to give to others. Love is the motive for everything that God does. God Himself is love, that is His essence. He chose to love – *"God is love."* (1 John 4:8).

The one who loves, always wants to be near their beloved. God's will is that we should always be with Him. That is why He labored throughout human history to bring us back into His presence. Trying to show us who He is, striving for us to know Him and see Him as He is. This is a heavy burden that He has been carrying since the creation of the world. This burden is the pain of separation from us and is heard throughout the Scriptures. This cry of His love was uttered for the first time at the dawn of history in the Garden of Eden to Adam, *"Where are you!"* (Genesis 3:9), and this cry peaked when He sent Jesus the

Messiah to die for us on the cross. This same cry opens the book of Malachi too, *"I have loved you," says the LORD* (Malachi 1:2).

The Love of God is the power that drives everything He does. *"For I know the thoughts that I think toward you", says the LORD, "thoughts of peace and not of evil, to give you a future and a hope"* (Jeremiah 29:11). This message comprises the basis for all of God's messages. The message of the love of God, is the first and foremost message that God seeks to convey and this is also the most important message for God's messengers. Knowing and understanding God's love is the basis for our relationship with Him and for the mission on which He sends us.

To what extent do you know and understand the love of God? Have you experienced the love of God or have you only heard of it? As God's messengers we were called to carry the burden of this message of His love to the world and to partake in His love. That means we must do as He does, love those that are hard for us to love, even those who hate us and those who are not so nice to us.

Only when we experience the depth of God's love towards ourselves, are we capable of passing this love on. In fact, our ability to love is directly dependent on how deep our experience of the love of God toward us is. Pray and ask God to show you His love. Do not be bashful, He wants to do it! Experiencing His love will free you to love others.

Day 5

"I have loved you," says the LORD. ***"Yet you say, 'In what way have You loved us?'"*** (Malachi 1:2).

God declaring His love to us causes an immediate reaction from us, just as it did from the children of Israel: *"In what way do You love us?"*. "You do not really love us! If You really loved us, You would have given us what we wanted. If You really loved me no difficult things would have happened to me. You would have given me the spouse I wanted, the job I do not have, the health that is failing me, and faithful friends." The complaints against God immediately bursts from our hearts in reaction to God's declaration of His love.

The wrong understanding that love means giving us everything we want, and not withholding from us anything that we consider a blessing, prevents us from accepting the fullness of God's love. This in turn prevents us from being faithful messengers of God.

Not understanding the fullness of God's love prevents us from receiving God's blessing. It deeply harms our relationship with God and with people, and damages our ministry and mission. If I myself do not know this deep love of God, how can I proclaim it to others?

There are a few things that hinder us from experiencing and enjoying God's love.

The first thing that hinders us is our past experiences. Most of us have not grown up in a warm and loving environment. The parents of many of us hurt us instead of protecting us, and we now project the image of our parents onto God and we think God is that way too. If God is our father, then He loves us like our father did. He too is short tempered, angry and spanks for no reason. He too reacts impulsively and capriciously. God too is never pleased with us and is cold and distant. We should remember that our father is sinful and flawed even if he had good intentions. And the image we have of him is based on that. This causes us to think that God the Father is the same way and this impairs our ability to accept God's love in its fullness. We were hurt in the past and we will not allow anyone, not even God to hurt us again.

One of the things that brought me much healing was, when I learned of the forgiveness that I must grant to people that hurt me, whether they asked for it or not. I understood that if God forgave me my great offences against Him, then I too must forgive the debt of people who hurt me (Matthew 18). I sat alone in my room and asked the Holy Spirit to show me those areas in my life where other people, my parents and especially my father had hurt me. Right away I started to remember incident after incident in which I was hurt to the depths of my soul. The pain was still there even though it was suppressed underneath the surface. One by one I lifted up every incident in prayer before God, and I said out loud:

"God, just as You pardoned my debt to you, and forgave my many offenses against You, I too, lift up _____ (here comes the name of the person) before you and forgive him/her for _____ (here comes a **short** description of the incident). I release them and their debt toward me. I let go of my demand for justice from them. Give me the strength to release them, and heal me please in the name of Jesus the Messiah who died for me and took my debt upon Himself."

As you remember incidents from your past and there is still pain; this means you have not yet forgiven, and that you are not free to receive God's love. This unforgiveness binds you.

Are you willing to allow God to release and heal the hurts you suffered from in the past, so that you can experience the depth of His love? Are you willing to give up the debt of revenge and judgment that they owe you? Are you ready to give up your right to revenge? Your right for justice? The wish to see the offender suffer as you did? Make those decisions while in prayer, and go through the process of forgiving the people that hurt you.

Day 6

"Yet you say, 'In what way have You loved us?'"
(Malachi 1:2).

Another thing that hinders us from experiencing God's love is our actions and especially the actions we hide from others. We keep private sins that we do not want to get rid of because somehow they give us pleasure. We justify impatient, angry or rude behavior as part of our personality. We justify this as a way in which we speak the truth in love, as something that distinguishes us from others. Another thing we do is that when we are in the company of believers we behave as believers, but when we are next to unbelievers we fit in and behave like them.

In Isaiah 59:1-2 it is written *"Behold, the LORD's hand is not shortened, that it cannot save; nor His ear heavy, that it cannot hear. But your iniquities have separated you from your God."* Our actions and the things we allow our thoughts and eyes to focus on, when they are contrary to the Word of God distance us from God and hinder us from experiencing the fullness of His love.

Every action has a consequence even if it is not seen immediately. Every in-action has a consequence. It was once said that what evil needs in order to flourish is that good people take no action to oppose it. What sin needs in order to bear fruit is that we will not resist it. Every seed bears fruit even if it is buried deep in the ground and is not seen for a long time.

Examine your actions, examine your thoughts. Are you doing things that you know are contrary to the Word of God? Do you let anger fill your heart and thoughts? The desire for revenge, for justice for yourself? Do you let unforgiveness take root in your heart or have bitterness against people for the way they have treated you? Do you have lustful thoughts? Do you allow your eyes to look at the intimate parts of others?

If we want to experience God's love, we must resist the sin ingrained in us and repent from our sinful actions and thoughts. We must bring them to the foot of the cross and leave them there. We must ask forgiveness and grant forgiveness. Sometimes we must also forgive ourselves as God has forgiven us.

Are you willing to repent of hidden actions and thoughts and hand them over to God today? Remember the story about the Pharisee and the tax collector in Luke 18:10-14. It is the tax collector who recognized his sin and confessed it, who went home justified.

Day 7

"Yet you say, 'In what way have You loved us?'" (Malachi 1:2).

When God created the world He looked at everything and determined that *"it is very good"*, but when we look in the mirror we say "God, this is not so good, with me, You have failed".
Psalms 139:5, 14 says: *"You have hedged me behind and before, and laid Your hand upon me... I will praise You, for I am fearfully and wonderfully made; marvelous are Your works, and that my soul knows very well."* David's soul knew that God made him unique and that he was wonderfully made. He knew that in all of history and in all the world there is not, was not and will not be anyone who is exactly like him. David knew that God made the effort, planned him and created him special and that is why he could say with all his heart *"marvelous are Your works, and that my soul knows very well."*

Because we adopt worldly standards of beauty, we are not happy with the way God made us. "If I had blue eyes I would be beautiful", "If I were thinner, taller, shorter, blond, black haired...." We compare ourselves to others and always find someone who is better than us. Because of this we point a blaming finger at God and say, "You might have created the whole world very good, but with me You could have done a bit better...". We are not satisfied with how God made us, and therefore we think deep in our hearts in the place where many times we dare not look "if He made such a mistake with me, how can I trust Him not to make other mistakes?".

Fashion always changes. In the middle ages a full woman was the symbol of perfect beauty. In the sixties Twiggy appeared, who was as her name suggests, as thin as a twig and she became the object of admiration for the daughters of Eve who tried to imitate her. But God does not work according to fashion. He does not change.

God knows what He is doing, and your body which serves as a frame for your soul, is perfect and was made in order to highlight God's special beauty of creation in you. The same way a beautiful frame highlights the painting that it is framing.

The question is: do I accept the fact that God did a good job creating me and thank Him for that as David did, or will I blame Him for the fact I am not beautiful/thin/tall such as _____? (Fill in the blank with any name you want to.)

If I cannot accept that God created me perfectly, I will not be able to experience the fullness of His love because I do not trust Him. What is your choice? Do you gladly accept the way you look? Can you thank God today for the way He made you? If so then do that and tell Him in prayer.

Day 8

"Yet you say, 'In what way have You loved us?'"
(Malachi 1:2).

In one way or another we all have an image of who God is, and when this image is incomplete or incorrect it affects our ability to accept His love.

Usually there are two images of God that most people have with minor variations – these reflect pictures that stem from our personal experience with figures of authority in our lives.

1.   **God the punisher.** In this image God is an angry God. He holds a stick in His hand and waits for us to make a mistake so that He can punish us. He loves to punish, and all those words about "God is love" are just a cover, a mask for us to come closer to Him so He can smack us. He is a cruel and proud God who loves people to grovel before Him. Only our suffering can appease Him.

2.   **The all embracing, "kind-hearted" God.** In this image, God is like an old man with a white beard who accepts everything we say and do without question or limitation. A type of Santa Claus who no matter what we did, will always say: "You've been a good boy. Here are you presents." No limits, everything is allowed and nothing is forbidden. He loves everybody and by this we mean that He accepts everybody regardless of how they live their lives. Stealing, lies and adultery do not matter, we can go on with our lifestyle as before and He will not

let anything come between us. There is no such thing as sin that separates us from God. Everyone will be with God at the end of the day seeing that God loves everybody."

When we hold a distorted image of who God is our ability to accept His love is limited as well, since everything that God does or says passes through these lenses we wear and is therefore distorted.

In order for things to change and our image of God to become more like the real thing, we must first forgive people with authority in our lives (like we did in day 5) and afterwards dare to come to God asking Him to show us and teach us who He really is. One of the scary things to do is to ask God to show us who He really is, because if we ask, then He might answer...

Do you have the courage to put all the images that you have of God aside and ask Him to show you who He really is? Do you have the courage to say to God like Moses: *"Please, show me Your glory"* (Exodus 33:18)? When He does that He will shatter many of our images of Him!
If you do have that courage, ask Him in prayer to show you who He really is.

Day 9

"Yet you say, 'In what way have You loved us?'" (Malachi 1:2).

A wrong understanding of what love is also preventing us from receiving God's true love in its fullness.
Since the world never shows us true love, and it is from there that we have learned what love is, our perception of love is faulty. Until God corrects our understanding and reveals to us what true love is, it will be difficult for us to understand His love and to receive it.

There are a few ways in which our perception of love is incorrect:

1. **Love is admiration.** We think that whoever loves us needs to admire us. The difference is that admiration does not see any shortcomings but rather only perfection, while true love, loves irrespective of the shortcomings. Therefore, whoever substitutes love with admiration is a very lonely person who will not allow people to come too close to him, thinking: "If they come too close they will truly know me, see my shortcomings and stop loving me."
Unfortunately, some of the leaders in the body of Messiah behave in this way and keep an "admiration distance" - a distance from the people they are leading out of fear that if the people truly knew them they would stop loving them and following them. True love knows the beloved truly and deeply with all his

or her faults, and yet still loves and is committed to love.

2.   **Love is giving attention.** Here the thought is that whoever loves us has to place us at the center of their lives, always making a fuss about us. We have to be the center of their attention. Such a person always seeks the attention of people around him, since attention is love. That is why there are so many people who want to be famous. If you are a celebrity, then you are always attracting attention and everyone loves you. "If you do not always pay attention to me, it means that you do not love me, since the world revolves around me!" Understand and embrace the fact that the world does not revolve around you, and love does not mean giving you constant attention.

3.   **Love means that the one who loves me will always give me what I want.** Many times it is the exact opposite. A parent who gives his child everything the child wants does not build him up but ruins him. If a parent loves his child he does not give him unlimited amounts of chocolate or anything else that will harm him, even if the child vehemently demands it. In such a situation love will express itself by not giving. A parent's role is not to be the servant of his children but to prepare them for life.

4.   **Love is protective and makes sure nothing bad will happen to me.** "If God loved me, He would not allow difficult and bad things to happen to me", we think. Hardship in our lives strengthens us, if we go through them in the right way. In the same way that resistance strengthens a muscle and a muscle without resistance degenerates, so it is with hardships in our lives. When we react to them

correctly by giving thanks to God and responding the way He would want us to, they strengthen us. If we react the wrong way, hardships crush us; if we react the right way they build us up.

The role of every parent, especially God as a perfect Father, is to give His children the tools to cope with life. A parent who admires his children and does not see their faults harms them. A parent who always puts his children at the center and gives them constant attention harms them because he teaches them that the world revolves around them. A parent who gives his children everything they want, tries to buy their love and in doing so harms them. A parent who shields his children from any difficulty and does not allow them experience hardships, harms them.

What should we do?

1. Forgive your parents and others who have hurt you. Express that forgiveness in Jesus name, speak it out in an audible voice.
2. Repent and ask God's forgiveness for actions, thoughts and wishes that are contrary to God.
3. Repent of the thought that the world revolves around you, from demanding that God meets your conditions before you serve Him, and from the thought that He is there to serve you.
4. Thank God for the way He made you, for the way you look.
5. Ask Him to reveal His love to you.

Day 10

"Yet Jacob I have loved; but Esau I have hated"
(Malachi 1:2-3).

When people think of love, they think of a special mysterious emotion that makes us want to be with the one we love. This mysterious emotion is the subject of many songs and poems that have been written over many centuries. Most people are looking for this mysterious feeling all their lives. Falling in love, and being in love have become life's goal for many people in the world. They go from one lover to the next in constant search for that exciting emotion, the emotion that always slowly fades away. When we read 1 Corinthians 13 which is called the 'Love Chapter', and wonderfully describes love, we do not find any reference to an emotion or feeling, but rather to actions.

According to the Scriptures, love is not a feeling, but a decision and action. Love is choosing and doing the very best for the one we love even if it comes at a cost to us.

God does not sit in heaven to delight Himself in some pleasant and mysterious emotion of love. He does what is best for us, even if we do not understand it. A good parent does not always do what feels pleasant and nice but what is good for his children. This is why he sometimes punishes them, not out of anger but out of love that seeks to improve, correct and build up his beloved children.

All the things that God does are good because they stem from His love – His knowledge and choice for what is best for us. When He tells us: *"you shall love your neighbor as yourself"* (Leviticus 19:18), He does not tell us to feel a warm fuzzy feeling toward someone, but to do for your neighbor what is best for him, even if it comes at a cost to you. Do not wait for feelings before you act, rather act and then maybe the feelings will come. Love is not a feeling. Love is choice and an action. Love is not a fuzzy and pleasant feeling that wells up in our heart and that stays inside us forever. Love is in our decisions and actions toward others. There is no love without actions.

Is it hard for you to feel love and affection toward certain people? That does not matter. Decide to act and do the best for them regardless of the emotions you feel.

"By this all will know that you are My disciples, if you have love for one another" (John 13:35). Acts of love not feelings of love.

Day 11

"Yet Jacob I have loved; but Esau I have hated" (Malachi 1:2-3).

Esau despised God's calling to be the firstborn of the family. He sold his birthright for the momentary pleasure of a warm stew. The result was that God dispossessed him not only from the birthright but from the blessing as well. Here we have a strong expression to describe what happened, it is written that God hated him. According to Wikipedia hatred is defined as "an extreme, deep and emotional dislike".

Does God hate? Does He have emotions of hatred? We know that God hates sin and here we are told that He hates a person, or a nation. We are told in Luke 14:26 that, *"If anyone comes to Me and does not hate his father and mother, wife and children, brothers and sisters, yes, and his own life also, he cannot be My disciple."* In Matthew 10:37, a parallel verse to the Luke verse, it's written, *"He who loves father or mother more than Me is not worthy of Me. And he who loves son or daughter more than Me is not worthy of Me."*

As we saw in yesterday's reading, love is not a feeling but rather a decision and action. Therefore, also God's hatred toward Esau or our hatred toward anyone who is more important to us than God, does not speak of feelings or emotions, but of decisions and the actions of rejecting those people's place in our lives.

We are told to reject and to be inwardly hostile towards putting anyone or anything higher than God. This is because loving anyone, or anything, more than God means making that person an idol that takes God's place in our lives. We must love God *"with all your heart, with all your soul, and with all your strength"* (Deuteronomy 6:5), and anything or anyone that we love more than Him distances us from Him. That is why we have to hate and battle any feeling or thought that causes us to love people or things more than God - Not to battle the people but our attitude towards them.

We must reject ourselves as being the center of the universe and we must put God in that place. We must reject and distance, in our actions not our emotions, anything that takes the place of God in the center of our lives. We must reject inside our hearts, inside our thoughts the ones we count as more important than God, while outwardly doing works of love toward them. We must reject placing them in God's place, but not reject them as people.

Is there something or someone that is more important to you than God? Hate them. This means; choose to reject them from their elevated place in your mind and heart, and give that place to the One it truly belongs to - to God. Be careful not to despise the calling and election of God, He chose Jacob and rejected Esau. Search your heart in prayer asking God to show you if you have allowed someone or something else to take His place in your life.

Day 12

"Yet Jacob I have loved; but Esau I have hated" (Malachi 1:2-3).

Does God treat different people differently? Does He discriminate against people?
Jacob with all his shortcomings listened to God, did as God told him and went where God led him. Jacob followed the faith of his father Isaac, even though he was far from perfect.
Esau, in contrast to him, did what he liked. Although he too grew up in a home where the Lord was worshipped, he did not care about his position in the home as the firstborn. He very easily gave up his place in God's family for the sake of fulfilling his bodily needs. In all of what he did we do not read of any relationship between him and God. In his actions he proved his hatred toward God by rejecting Him, and therefore God rejected him too.

When I came to faith, those who taught me, told me that God does not have favorites, and that He treats everyone the same way. This verse like other verses shows that they were wrong.

In Psalm 4:3 it is written: *"But know that the LORD has set apart for Himself him who is godly;"*, the word in Hebrew for *'set apart'* is the same word as *'to discriminate'*. God definitely discriminates in favor of those who belong to Him. He treats us differently than He treats those who do not believe in Him, especially those like Esau who knew about Him and rejected Him.

God is not fair, He is merciful. If He was fair, we would all get the punishment we deserve. Merriam-Webster dictionary defines fair as "treating people in a way that does not favor some over others" God treats those who belong to Him differently to those who do not belong to Him. He hears our prayers and answers them all the time, He protects and keeps us, He leads and directs us, He fulfills our needs, He saved us, He sanctifies and purifies us and molds us into His image. To the believers He says, *"I will never leave you nor forsake you."* (Hebrews 13:5). Not so to the non-believers. *"And we know that all things work together for good to those who love God, to those who are the called according to His purpose"* (Romans 8:28). The way God treats us is not the way He treats those who do not believe. If that is not discrimination, then I do not know what discrimination is.

God's desire is that everyone will belong to Him so that He can treat them differently, but in practice it does not happen. God does discriminate in favor of those who belong to Him. God discriminates in your favor. Thank Him for the special way He sees you and treats you.

Day 13

*Your eyes shall see, and you shall say, '**The LORD is magnified beyond the border of Israel**'* (Malachi 1:5).

One of the difficulties for the children of Israel was seeing God as the God of the whole world, and not only as the God of Israel and of the Land of Israel. The writer of Psalm 137 expressed this perceived relationship between the God of Israel and Land of Israel in verse 4 *"How can we sing the LORD's song in a foreign land?"* In Israel's view the two, God and the Land of Israel cannot be separated. Identifying the Lord as the God of Israel is good and right, since He Himself presents Himself this way, but at the same time God is the God of all the earth.

Our immediate response is: "Of course I know that God is the God of all the earth!" But we ignore the fact that the tendency to limit God to the confinements of what we know is not just a tendency that the children of Israel had at that time, but it is our tendency as well. Since we find it comfortable within the borders of what we know we also tend to limit the Lord to our ability to understand Him. We think the Lord is like us and that He acts like us and thinks like we do. God is much greater than our understanding. When we limit Him to our understanding of Him, that is exactly what we do – we limit Him.

One of God's works in our lives is to shatter and stretch the limits of our understanding. Each time we think we understand Him, He does things differently and shows us how little we understand about Him. In the gospels we see that nearly every time Jesus was asked to heal He laid hands on the sick, but when they asked Him to lay His hands on the sick He did something different – He spat, made mud and spread it on the eyes of the blind man; He put His fingers in the ears of the deaf man etc. God seeks again and again to demonstrate to us that He does not act according to our will and understanding. He is magnified beyond our borders of understanding.

God is the God of all the earth, and His will is that we know that He is magnified beyond our borders as well, beyond our understanding, beyond our thoughts. *"For My thoughts are not your thoughts, nor are your ways My ways," says the LORD. "For as the heavens are higher than the earth, so are My ways higher than your ways, and My thoughts than your thoughts." (Isaiah 55:8-9).*

Do you have the courage to tell God, "God, show me who You really are! Break the boundaries of my understanding of You, stretch them - be magnified beyond my borders."? Are you truly ready for Him to show you? If you are, then ask Him to do it.

Day 14

"A son honors his father, and a servant his master. If then I am the Father, where is My honor? And if I am a Master, where is My reverence? Says the LORD of hosts to you priests who despise My name." (Malachi 1:6)

God has complaints against those who are supposed to serve and represent Him. They disgrace God by the way they relate to Him. We notice that God does not yet reprimand them for their behavior, but for their attitude towards Him – they do not honor Him and do not revere Him.

Let us remember again that everything that God does stems from His burden of love. He does not want to blame; He wants to correct. He wants to put right that which is twisted and corrupt, so that His love can flow freely to those who belong to Him and so that they will be in constant intimacy with Him. That is why He rebukes – to correct.

In order for that to happen He first concentrates on correcting attitudes and approaches - the things inside a man's heart that determine his behavior, before He corrects the behavior of those who belong to Him.

Religion begins by attempting to alter man's behavior, hoping that change of conduct will cause a change of approach, attitude of the heart and thoughts. Religion claims that changing the external behavior will change the inner man. God on the other hand when building the tabernacle in the desert starts with the inside and works His way out. He changes the heart, and then as a result of that the behavior changes. God first changes the attitudes and approach.

God does not seek that we glorify and fear Him in order to build Himself up. He does not need it – He is perfect. His desire is that we honor and fear Him because only then will we truly know our place, who we are and especially – who He is. In His great love He wants us to come closer to Him and to always be with Him. For this to happen our attitude toward Him needs to be correct. Attitude before works.

Jesus Himself spoke about those who would perform wonders in His name, speak great things in His name and do great things - but He does not even know them (Matthew 7:21-23). Their works and their speech were "right" but did not stem from honoring God and fearing Him but rather from a desire to build themselves up and to become famous. They thought that the way to glorify God was for themselves to become respected and famous (exactly the opposite of what Malachi did). This thing should cause fear in the heart of everyone who serves God because this attitude is prevalent in the Christian world. Many believers think they can glorify God more if they themselves become more famous. So serving God becomes a way to make themselves more famous. The more famous and well known I become, the more I can glorify God they reason, God is looking for the attitude of the heart not for works. God is looking for a humble heart not a famous person. Malachi understood that.

What is the attitude of your heart in God's service? Are you seeking glory for yourself? Do you think that the more people recognize you the better you can serve God? Do you try to take some of God's honor for yourself? *"If then I am the Father, where is My honor? And if I am a Master, where is My reverence?"*
Ask God to help you honor Him in the right way, seeking His glory not yours.

Day 15

"A son honors his father, and a servant his master. If then I am the Father, where is My honor? And if I am a Master, **where is My reverence** *(in Hebrew - fear)? Says the LORD of hosts to you priests who despise My name."* (Malachi 1:6)

In my opinion, one of the words that is least understood is 'fear'. Proverbs 9:10 says: *"The fear of the LORD is the beginning of wisdom"* and therefore it is important for those who are seeking wisdom, those who are seeking to relate to the Lord in the right way to fear Him. The word 'fear' means being afraid, this is what the word means in Hebrew. It is hard for us to understand how this works, since it is also written *"There is no fear in love"* (1 John 4:18). If the beginning of wisdom is the fear of God, and God wants us to be wise, this means that God does indeed want us to fear Him, but it also says there is no fear in love... What does it mean?

Fear is not a bad thing in itself. What is bad; is the fear of things we should not fear or fearing too much the things we should fear little. A healthy fear is a mechanism that God has given us in order to protect us. The corruption and distortion of that fear came about as a result of sin. Corrupted fear is a bad thing, but originally fear is a good thing. We should be afraid to walk off the roof, or put our hand into a fire, we should be afraid to sin.

When we work with fire or with electricity we fear them. That does not mean we think that fire and electricity are bad, but we understand that we must treat them appropriately and that incorrect treatment of fire or electricity will harm us. This is healthy fear.

I am not comparing God to electricity, but I am comparing the fear we have of electricity to the fear of God. When we handle electricity or fire we think before every action we take, and try to foresee what result it might have. So should the fear of the Lord cause us to calculate our thoughts and deeds before we execute them to determine what effect they may have on our relationship with God. Only when we understand that a certain action will have good results from God's perspective should we do it. The fear of the Lord is the beginning of wisdom because it causes us to think about the consequences of the things we do before we do them. Fear of the Lord is not just honor or respect, as many people present it. True fear of the Lord is honor mixed with fear. Not the type of fear that causes us to run away but the type of fear that causes us to think about the consequences of the things we do and think. We must honor God and fear Him.

Ask God to help you to fear Him today. This is the beginning of wisdom.

Day 16

"Yet you say, 'In what way have we despised Your name?'" (Malachi 1:6)

In Malachi we see God's people claiming again and again that they have no idea what He is talking about – He is accusing them of things that are not true (see 1:2, 6, 7, 2:14, 17, 3:7, 13). "We? What are you talking about? You probably mean someone else, not me... I'm ok, it is the others who are not". The scripture in John 3:19-20 was true then and is still true today. *"... the light has come into the world, and men loved darkness rather than light, because their deeds were evil. For everyone practicing evil hates the light and does not come to the light, lest his deeds should be exposed."* When we read these verses we immediately ascribe them to those who are not believers. By doing this we make a mistake. God's reproof is directed first and foremost to those whom He loves and who belong to Him, to the believers who represent Him.

Our ability to play innocent, to excuse and hide the truth about ourselves from others and even from ourselves, is amazing. We cover up things inside ourselves. We behave in public like spiritual people but when we are alone we cultivate lustful thoughts, look at pictures or movies that arouse sinful lusts, take to ourselves honor that belongs only to God, think we are better than others, use the Word of God and our "spirituality" to obtain a place of respect for ourselves and to obtain benefits from others. We hurt others who appear to be a threat to our position - and so on and so on and so on...

In John 16:7-8, Jesus promises to send the Holy Spirit to the Believers. The work of the Spirit is to convict the Believers of sin, of righteousness and of judgment. The rebuke for these things is intended first and foremost for the believers who belong to God and who represent Him in this world. They are His messengers seeing that the Spirit was given to them.

In James 1:22-25 it is written that the Word of God is like a mirror that by the light of the Holy Spirit shows us who we really are. Our avoidance of our own ugliness and our attempt to forget and hide who we really are does not hide the truth from God. In any dispute between the Word of God and ourselves, the Word of God is always right and we are always wrong.

To be a faithful messenger of God, I must accept His Word as absolute truth. I must read it every day and ask Him to expose the hidden things of my heart, the things I hide from myself, the things I do not see and do not want to see. Do you have the courage to open your heart before God and ask Him to show you the truth about yourself, or do you argue with Him when He tries to correct you? Remember that everything He does stems from His love!

Day 17

"Yet you say, 'In what way have we despised Your name?'" (Malachi 1:6)

If you do not want a direct answer from God, you better not ask Him a direct question. They ask, *"In what way have we despised You?"*, and to their surprise God begins to give the details.

God has a list of things He wants to correct, and those who belong to Him and who want to be His messengers must give Him a free hand to change them. Those of us who want to be faithful messengers of God have to take this list seriously and listen.

When we come to faith, God exchanges our stony hearts for a heart of flesh and puts His Spirit within us. (Ezekiel 36) Unfortunately in our hardness of heart we allow hard areas to remain in our lives, areas that resist God. The Scriptures call it *"stubbornness of heart*"*, where the Hebrew for *stubbornness* shares the same root as the word *muscle* – that is – we walk in the muscle, in the strength of our heart. The process of growing in God is a process in which God unveils area after area in our hearts where our heart is hard and then softens it – if we allow Him to soften it. Because of His love for

---

*   *" 'Yet they did not obey or incline their ear, but walked, each one, in the stubbornness of his evil heart; therefore I brought on* them *all the words of this covenant, which I commanded them to do, but they did not.' "* (Jeremiah 11:8, NASB)

us, God does not show us all the hard areas in our hearts at once, but rather does this gradually according to our ability to receive instruction and to cooperate with Him. He starts with the bigger areas and with time He moves to smaller and smaller areas. The process starts when we come to faith and continues for the duration of our lives. God's purpose is to purify to Himself a holy people who faithfully represent Him in the world.

God does not expose sin and shine His light on the hardness of our hearts because He wants to shame or accuse us, but because of His love for us He wants to remove from our lives anything that hinders us from deeper intimacy with Him. He only does this work with our cooperation. He does not force us to give up the hardness of our heart but asks us anew each time, "Will you allow me to soften you?" Many times when we think of the pain involved in shattering the rocky places of our hearts we are afraid and resist. When this happens God stops His work and waits for our consent. We cannot sanctify and purify ourselves. However, we can cooperate with Him in the work of sanctification and purification that He desires for us by softening our hearts and agreeing both in advance, and with each new day for Him to do His work within us in whatever way He pleases, whenever He pleases, and wherever He pleases to do it.

Whoever wants to be a faithful messenger of God must partner with Him in His work and cooperate with Him.

Decide to cooperate with Him, and tell Him that you are ready for Him to do His work of breaking the hard areas in you today and every day.

Day 18

"You offer defiled food (Hebrew – Bread) **on My altar**, *but say, 'In what way have we defiled You?' By saying, 'The table of the LORD is contemptible.'* (Malachi 1:7)

The showbread that was placed on the table in the Holy Place of the Tabernacle, symbolizes the Word of God which must be regularly "eaten" by those who belong to God. It is illuminated by the light of the candlestick, the Menorah which is the light of the Holy Spirit. As those who serve God as a kingdom of priests we too must feed daily from His Word in the light of the Holy Spirit. The first thing that God shows those who belong to Him is; that they are disrespectful towards His Word and therefore the bread they serve to others is defiled.

The tendency in these modern days is to try and make things user-friendly and this include the Scriptures. People look for an easy-read, an understanding that does not require any effort with immediate sanctification. But the Word of God both Old and New Covenants are not intended for quick reading and ease of use. It is intended for "rock shattering" (Jeremiah 23:29) and *"division of ... joints and marrow"* (Hebrews 4:12).

Many believers in the world today do not know the Scriptures well because the emphasis today is not on desiring to understand the source better, but on making reading it easy. The requirement for readers searching the Scriptures (1 Peter 1:10) is to understand the intention of the writer and adapt themselves to it, this is not required anymore. Rather than adapting the readers to the Scriptures, there is an attempt to simplify and adapt the Scriptures to the readers. The Word of God is no longer that important but rather the ability of the reader to read it easily and fluently. This is the reason behind many of the translations published today.

This has led to a situation where in many churches the borders are not clear any more. Divorce is accepted even among leaders. Female pastors and living together before marriage is becoming widespread. Disrespecting the Word of God and attempting to adapt it to "modern life" disgraces the Lord, and consequently the things we learn and teach as God's messengers become defiled.

As believers the written Word of God has to receive the respect that is due to it and it must be the main authority in our lives. The Word of God does not adapt itself to us or to changing fashions. It is like God who gave it *"the same yesterday and today and forever "*(Hebrews 13:8). We are the ones that should adapt ourselves to it and not try to adapt the Word of God to modern times.

Do you make an effort to adapt yourself to the Word of God, or do you try to adapt the Word of God to yourself? Do you need to repent?

Day 19

*"**And when you offer the blind as a sacrifice, is it not evil? And when you offer the lame and sick, is it not evil?** Offer it then to your governor! Would he be pleased with you? Would he accept you favorably?" Says the LORD of hosts.* (Malachi 1:8)

God's requirement for who can serve Him as a priest, and what sacrifices can be made are detailed and exact. The priest must be healthy and without deformity and so should the sacrifice. They must fulfill the requirements of God in the Scriptures.

In most churches of the world until not so many years ago, the requirements of those who were ministers of God in the church were clear. Church pastors and elders were always men (2 Timothy 2:12 for instance), people of good reputation, married to one wife, sober, self-controlled, well mannered, hospitable and able to teach (1 Timothy 3:2). They were people who reflected the Messiah in their character.

In recent years there has been an increasing gnawing away at the criteria that the Scriptures dictate because of the attempt to adapt the Scriptures to modern society, and make the church more user-friendly. Our emotions and the desire to be like society around us causes us to adapt the church and God's requirements for those who serve Him, to suit our society. Instead of trying to influence the society to change and adopt the criteria of the Scriptures, we open the doors for women to lead the church, for divorcees to serve in holy things, and for people who live together without being married to hand out the Lord's supper. We do not ask people anymore how they live their lives, what their relationships are like with their wives or if there is pornography in their lives. We open the doors of ministry in the church to just about anyone. Are you musically talented? Come and lead the worship! Do you know how to speak well? Come and teach! Do you have charisma? Good – then come and be a leader! Character that does not reflect the Messiah? No matter... A sinful life? Never mind... When believers in the Messiah are represented by people who serve themselves, those who are seeking to become rich with money, fame, power and are motivated by their charisma, it is no wonder that churches in the world look the way they do. It is no wonder that we are no testimony to the world around us.

Will we who desire to be faithful messengers, those who want to represent the Messiah honorably, those who want to be messengers of the Lord – will we adapt ourselves to His word and will and give offerings that are in accordance with His will and requirements; or will we continue to try to be liked by the people around us? *"Entreat God's favor"* (Malachi 1:9), seek His presence, seek Him and His will. Are you and the sacrifices that you offer in accordance with God's criteria, or do you not care if these criteria are not clear in your life? A faithful messenger must represent the one that sends him faithfully and clearly.

Day 20

"Who is there even among you who would shut the doors, so that you would not kindle fire on My altar in vain (Hebrew –for free)***?*** *I have no pleasure in you," says the Lord of hosts, "nor will I accept an offering from your hands."* (Malachi 1:10)

The Hebrew for *in vain* in this verse means *for free*. The reproof here is sharp and sadly applicable to most believers today. God reproves those who serve Him in order to gain something from it, those who serve Him to gain benefits.

He extends a challenge to them while asking: "Which of you would do His ministry without wanting to receive something in return?!"

Each one of us has a motive for serving God. In fact, most of us, if not all of us have a few layers of motives. I remember a period when I used to pray so that people would hear me and think I am spiritual, while at the same time thinking that if God answered my prayers – that would be nice. The reward I received was not that I fellowshipped with God but rather that people esteemed me more highly (that is what I thought). There are people who play music at church because they love playing music and at church they can develop their talent, there are people who help others because they like it when people need them and thank them, and there are those who minister for the sake of gaining recognition, power and influence or so that they can travel abroad, receive donations and so on and so on.

The question we all need to ask ourselves is; why am I doing what I am doing in the Kingdom of God? What are my motives? Am I willing to serve God without receiving anything in return? What do I think I will be gaining from it, or getting in return?

God wants us to serve Him only out of love. That the motive for all our works will be one – to be near to Him. *"You shall love the Lord your God with all your heart, with all your soul, and with all your strength"* (Deuteronomy 6:5, Matthew 22:37).

Today's verse (Mal. 1:10) says clearly that God has no pleasure in people who seek reward for their ministry other than drawing closer to God, and that He does not accept their sacrifice. This means that what they are doing is unacceptable to Him just as Cain's sacrifice was not accepted. Scary...!

We must have the fear of the Lord. We must bring our motives to God's light, repent and ask Him to correct them and then align ourselves with the only motive that God indeed does accept, the love of God. Examine your heart and see what your motive is. Are you motivated by trying to gain something for yourself through serving God? Is your love for God the only motive for serving Him? As we have mentioned; a good and faithful messenger has to represent the one that sends him, faithfully.

Day 21

"... Nor will I accept an offering from your hands. For from the rising of the sun, even to its going down, My name shall be great among the Gentiles; In every place incense shall be offered to My name, And a pure offering; For My name shall be great among the nations," *Says the Lord of hosts.* (Malachi 1:10-11)

This is an amazing declaration! It is in the TANACH (Old Covenant)! The name of God is great not only in Israel but also among the Gentiles. In every place upon the face of the earth He is offered incense, a pure offering; this is a declaration that is very hard for Israel to hear.

Apart from this amazing declaration, there is another saying here that directly offends our hearts, our pride, the place where we think that we are the center of the world. God says something here to the children of Israel and to the priests that is very unpleasant to hear: "I do not need you. I do not want your offerings. And I would like you to know that all over the world, people – Gentiles – whom you look down upon and think that you are better than them, offer me pure sacrifices that are better than your sacrifices." God is telling the children of Israel and those who serve Him that the very ones they consider enemies and inferior, offer the Lord a better sacrifice than they do.

This reminds us of the story from Luke 18:10-14 about the Pharisee and the tax collector who both went up to the temple. The Pharisee compared himself to the tax collector, told God how much better he is than the tax collector and took pride in the fact that he proves his love toward God by the deeds he performs. The tax collector just pounded his chest, confessed that he is a sinner and asked for forgiveness.

Many of us see our works as a proof of the measure of our love towards God. Most of us, if not all of us, compare ourselves constantly to others in order to measure our spirituality. We prefer to compare ourselves to unspiritual people because this helps us feel better about ourselves.

God's message is very clear – I do not need you! I love you and want you, but I do not need you. Do not think you are better than others, and that for this reason I will accept your offerings. Those whom you esteem lesser, even your enemies, offer a pure sacrifice while you do not.

Are there people you look down on thanking God that you are better than them? Arabs? Gentiles? Coarse Israeli Sabras? Be careful and repent! Make sure your offering is pure without paying attention to what is going on with other people's offerings.

Day 22

"You also say, 'Oh, what a weariness!' and you sneer at it," *says the Lord of hosts.* ***"And you bring the stolen, the lame, and the sick; Thus you bring an offering!*** *Should I accept this from your hand?" says the Lord.* (Malachi 1:13)

The picture portrayed here is of a child who when his parent asks him for something, breathes loudly and exclaims a long "Argh!" to express his dissatisfaction with his parent's request. Then instead of doing what the parent asked wholeheartedly, he only goes through the motions. He does not give his best and ends up doing less than what was requested. Clearly the behavior of a spoiled child.

A spoiled child thinks the world revolves around him and that his parent's duty is to entertain him, to ensure no hardships come his way, and to make sure he will not be bored. Sadly, believers also think God's duty is to take care of them, protect them, make sure nothing difficult happens to them and supply them with exciting entertainment in the form of miracles and wonders – every day, all day. Those people go from conference to conference to look for a thrill, seeking to escape hardships which they always ascribe to the Devil. These people are usually not a regular and stable part in a local church. Some of them attend several churches simultaneously that is, if they attend church at all. Others view the television or internet as their church, since no church is good enough for them. They always find fault with every church, and very quickly get fed up with that church. They view the church as a place that needs to give them something, rather than a place where they must give. Their reasons are always very "spiritual".

Do you also think that the church's role is to serve you? To give something to you? To give you thrills and excitement? Do you also think that God's duty is to protect you so that no hardships or difficulties will come your way? Are you also a spoiled child?

God's messengers were called to serve, not to be served. That is why we are called God's slaves. This is what both the Hebrew and Greek text say, slaves of God not servants of God. As God's slaves we must always seek to serve and to give, and not to take and receive. Do you view the church as a place where you should receive instead of as a place where you should give?

We can influence the church and the world much more, and we can grow in the Lord much more if we stop acting like spoiled children who think everything revolves around them. We should rather start to be God's slaves, serving both God and others in every place we find ourselves.
What about you? Is no church good enough for you? Are you seeking to give in church or are you looking for a church that gives to you? When God does not do things the way you want it, do you cry and complain? Does your life revolve around God or around yourself?

Day 23

*"But **cursed be the deceiver** who has in his flock a male, and takes a vow, but sacrifices to the Lord what is blemished— **for I am a great King**," Says the Lord of hosts, "and My name is to be feared among the nations."* (Malachi 1:14)

God is a king and we must treat Him as a king. He is not only a king who resides outside of us, He is a great king who dwells inside of us and demands control over all areas of His kingdom. Does God control all of you, or are there places where you have not yet enthroned Him – places that you keep for yourself? If you are still the one who is telling God where to reign and where not to, who is then the true ruler?

God, the great King has requirements; whoever tries to deceive Him and give Him less than what is required (one the prophet calls a *deceiver*) manages perhaps to deceive himself by believing that He is giving something to God, but he does not deceive God and his gift is not accepted.

Abel gave God a sacrifice according to God's will and his sacrifice was accepted. Cain gave what he wanted, and even when it came from the best of his fields his sacrifice was not accepted.

God has clear requirements: all or nothing. The best or nothing. His way or our way. Everything belongs to Him or nothing belongs to Him. We cannot give God a little or just a part of our lives. We cannot walk both in His ways and ours. We cannot give God some of our life or some of our will, some of our dreams and some of our money. God requires everything; if we are not willing to give Him everything then He accepts nothing. I am not saying that we will always manage to live this way and give all to God, but the decision has to be made and the battle against the flesh that resists this decision has to be fought.

Thus says the Lord: "Cursed is the man who trusts in man and makes flesh his strength, whose heart departs from the Lord. For he shall be like a shrub in the desert, and shall not see when good comes, but shall inhabit the parched places in the wilderness, in a salt land which is not inhabited. Blessed is the man who trusts in the Lord, and whose hope is the Lord. For he shall be like a tree planted by the waters, which spreads out its roots by the river, and will not fear when heat comes; But its leaf will be green, and will not be anxious in the year of drought, nor will cease from yielding fruit." (Jeremiah 17:5-8)

The choice is in our hands. If we choose to give all, the best to God, we will belong to Him totally, be part of His kingdom and be blessed. If we try to give Him less than He requires we will deceive ourselves and be accursed.
What do you choose? Tell Him your choice in prayer.

Day 24

*"And now, **O priests, this commandment is for you. If you will not hear, and if you will not take it to heart, to give glory to My name,** says the Lord of hosts, **"I will send a curse upon you, and I will curse your blessings.** Yes, I have cursed them already, **because you do not take it to heart."*** (Malachi 2:1-2)

God emphasizes that He is not speaking to those who do not believe in Him but to the priests who represent Him and are supposed to serve Him. He speaks to the priestly kingdom, to us – the believers.

God puts before us the blessing and the curse and requires us to choose. He tells us that in order for us to be blessed, we must obey Him and pay attention to fulfill our duty to glorify Him. The blessing will turn into a curse if we do not pay attention to our duty.

Taking to heart or paying attention means according to Merriam-Webster "The act or power of carefully thinking about, listening to, or watching someone or something : notice, interest, or awareness : special care or treatment"*

Once we stop focusing on God and paying the highest attention to Him, we move away from the blessing and receive the curse.

---

* http://www.merriam-webster.com/dictionary/attention

Blessing means, that we live out the fullness of what God created us for and prepared us for. God created each one of us special and with a special plan for us. Only when we live according to what God created us for, according to His plan for our lives, are we blessed. One that God created with a musical talent will not be blessed and fulfilled if he works in construction; another whom He has created with a love for mechanics or for woodwork will not be fulfilled playing musical instruments. Full blessing is found only when we live in the fullness of God's plan for us, the plan which He has prepared for us and for which He created us.

Curse is lack of blessing, like darkness is lack of light. The less light there is the greater the darkness. The further one wanders from blessing the greater the curse.

The Hebrew word for 'blessing' shares the same root as the word 'knee' or 'knees' (the Hebrew letters *bet, resh, kaph*). The only way to live in God's blessing is on your knees. Only when we bow the knee before the King of Kings, receiving His plan and will while remaining on our knees before Him, will we live in blessing. Anything else causes us to grow further from Him and intensifies the curse in our lives.
Decide to live your life on your knees before Him. Ask for His help to live this way.

Day 25

*"Then you shall know that **I have sent this commandment to you, that My covenant with Levi may continue**," says the Lord of hosts.* (Malachi 2:4)

God is a God of covenants. All of His relationships with people throughout history are based on covenants. A covenant is a contract and God is always faithful to every covenant He made. Most covenants include conditions that are required of people, and the blessings that God will grant if the covenant is kept or the curses that will come as a result of breaking the covenant. There are also unconditional covenants such as the covenant with Abraham or with David, in which God made no requirements, only promises.

When we sign a contract we commit to certain conditions and in return we receive certain things. If we violate a contract, there are consequences. Seeing that God takes His covenants seriously, He requires us to take the covenants we have with Him and with other people seriously too. In this passage God starts to reprove His nation because they are not faithful to the different covenants that they are a part of. As always He starts with the *"house of God"* (1 Peter 4:17), with the people who are called to serve Him and represent Him. God starts by reminding those who serve Him, His messengers, that He made a covenant with them. They entered into a relationship with Him in which He makes demands from them, and He is always faithful to them. If you gave your life to God, and you belong to Him you are part of the sons of Levi who were called to serve God and be His messengers. God signed this covenant with the blood of the Messiah, and He will always remain faithful to you. He will always stand by your side and will always do what is best for you.

God is always faithful to His covenant even when we are not. He is the One who said, *"I will never leave you nor forsake you"* (Hebrews 13:5, quoting Deuteronomy 31:6, 8). The same One who is faithful to the people of Israel despite our many sins is faithful to you too.

Do you know that He is with you always? Do you know that He always does what is best for you, even if you do not understand it? Do you know that He is always faithful to you? If you do, thank Him for it. If you do not, ask Him to open the eyes of your heart to know it, and choose to be faithful to the covenants that you are a part of.

Day 26

"Behold, I will rebuke your descendants and spread refuse on your faces, the refuse of your solemn feasts; And one will take you away with it. *Then you shall know that I have sent this commandment to you, that My covenant with Levi may continue," says the Lord of hosts.* (Malachi 2:3-4)

First of all, let us take notice of the Hebrew word play in this verse: *'descendants'/zera* and *'spread'/zariti, which sound the same; 'refuse on your faces'* and *'refuse of your solemn feasts' that repeat the same word*. This is in order to emphasize what is said.

The consequence of breaking the covenants that we are a part of is, that we come under a curse. Curses like blessings passes on to our seed *"to the third and the fourth generation"*, as is written in the Torah (Exodus 34:7).

It is important for us to understand that every decision and everything we do bears fruit and has consequences. If we live our lives on our knees in the presence of the great and awesome King, our works, our family and our children will be affected by it. If we move away from God and do not live our lives fully submitted to Him the results will be seen in our works, in our family and in all of our relationships. Even if the result is not seen immediately on the surface it will eventually come to light and be seen. The result of moving away from God is that our seed suffers and that God punishes the works of our hands.

The word for *refuse* means the rubbish that is left after offering the sacrifice. People who do not give God the first place in their lives but continue to give only an offering for the solemn feasts continue to behave as though they belong to God, but instead of their offering being accepted, God says that He will smear the refuse, the dirt, on their faces.

When Moses was in the presence of God, *"his face shone"* (Exodus 34:29-35). His face reflected the light of God and the people of Israel saw it. When we do not give God His rightful place as Lord, our face is covered with refuse and that is seen as well. We need only to look at people in the street to see the sadness, the depression and the darkness on their faces. The equivalent Hebrew saying for "His life is in the dumps" uses the same word as "rubbish" or "refuse" and we can see that in people's faces.

The reason God allows peoples' lives to be in the dumps; is to draw their attention. God made a covenant with us and His faithfulness to us is part of His covenant. He will not allow us to drift too far from Him without our noticing it. He allows the fruit of our lives, the consequences of our works to be seen in our family and also in us. He allows our lives to be in the dumps so that we can take notice, remember our covenant with Him and come back to honoring Him and fearing Him as a great and awesome God. He tries to get our attention. Only He can break the curse so that it will not continue to the next generations.

How does your life look? What kind of seeds are you sowing? Is the fruit in your life good or bad? How are your relationships with the people closest to you? Are there areas in your life that are in the dumps? Areas where the fruit is not the produce of blessing?
If there are some areas and relationships in your life that are in the dumps, do you make sure that you honor God in them? Is He totally Lord of your life and choices? Pay attention to these things, repent where necessary and straighten your walk.

"Keep your heart with all diligence, for out of it spring the issues of life" (Heb. "for from it are the results of life"). (Proverbs 4:23)

Day 27

"My covenant was with him, one of life and peace, and I gave them to him that he might fear Me; So he feared Me and was reverent before My name."
(Malachi 2:5)

Explaining what the curse was that followed unfaithfulness and the consequences thereof, He then speaks of the consequences of life being in covenant with God and emphasizes again the role of the messenger of the Lord. When the one serving God lives according to the covenant with God, the first consequence is that he has life and peace. The closer he draws to God the more peace and life grows in his life.

Life and death are not like black and white; they are more like light and darkness. The more you move away from the light the greater the darkness. The more one moves away from the Fountain of Life the more death abounds. *"In Him was life, and the life was the light of men"* (John 1:4). The closer we draw to Him the more we have life, and the further we move away from Him more death will abound in us. Entering into a covenant with God means entering into life. It This happens only when we come according to His desire and will. Entry into life is just the beginning of the process of drawing closer to Him the Fountain of Life, and for receiving more and more life and peace.

Peace with God can only be made when we take upon ourselves His way and will, when we honor Him and enthrone Him as the great God and King in our lives. This peace soaks into our thoughts and the things that we do.

Once we have entered into covenant with Him, He begins to give us glimpses of His glory - He reveals to us more and more of who He is, in order that we may draw nearer and receive more life and peace. The more we know Him and understand who He is, the more we fear Him. The more we fear Him the wiser we become and the closer we will draw to Him.

"...and I gave them to him that he might fear Me; So he feared Me and was reverent before My name." The fear of the Lord is a gift that God gives. The fear of God is a good thing because it makes us wiser and brings us closer to Him. Do not be afraid of the fear of God. The more fear of God we have, the more we will have peace and life. **"Every good gift and every perfect gift is from above, and comes down from the Father of lights, with whom there is no variation or shadow of turning."** (James 1:17)

Ask God to give you a greater fear of Him. In this way you will draw closer to Him and be filled with life and peace. You will then be a better messenger for Him.

Day 28

"My covenant was with him, one of life and peace, and I gave them to him that he might fear Me; So he feared Me and was reverent before My name. **The law of truth was in his mouth, and injustice was not found on his lips. He walked with Me in peace and equity** (Hebrew: mishor/integrity)**, and turned many away from iniquity. For the lips of a priest should keep knowledge, and people should seek the law from his mouth; For he is the messenger of the Lord of hosts.***"* (Malachi 2:5-7)

In these verses we find a list of things that are expected of the Lord's messenger, one that represents Him and lives in His covenant. If we want to be faithful messengers of God, we should take notice of the characteristics of the mission to which God is calling us.

The characteristics of the Lord's faithful messenger are: 1. The law of truth is in his mouth. 2. Injustice is not found on his lips. 3. He walks with God in peace. 4. He walks with God in integrity. 5. He turns many away from iniquity. 6. His lips keep knowledge. 7. People seek the law from his mouth.

1. **The law of truth is in his mouth.** He teaches the Word of God with faithfulness from the source. The Scriptures are the foundation upon which his teaching is built. In order for this to be true, he needs to know the Word of God (the Old and New Covenants) thoroughly. He must delve into the

Scriptures daily. *"This Book of the Law shall not depart from your mouth, but you shall meditate in it day and night, that you may observe to do according to all that is written in it. For then you will make your way prosperous, and then you will have good success."* (Joshua 1:8) He does not try to adapt the Scriptures to modern life but rather tries to adapt modern life to the Word of God. He speaks the truth. If he does not understand something he does not pretend to, but admits it. He teaches others the Word of God, he distributes the Word of God and he is not afraid to point out the truth to people around him. He does not allow the fear of what people may think of him to affect him. He teaches faithfully about Jesus who said: *"I am the way, the truth and the life"* (John 14:6).

2.   Injustice is not found on his lips. It is very important for the Lord's messenger to tell the truth, while trying with all his might not to hurt people. He does not gossip about people not even under the guise of "prayer requests". He does not tell people things that will hurt other people, he does not lie and he does not exaggerate. God's messenger thinks before he speaks - what will be the affect of his words upon the people around him? *"Who is the man who desires life, and loves many days, that he may see good? Keep your tongue from evil, and your lips from speaking deceit."* (Psalm 34:12-13)

3.   *He walked with Me in peace.* Peace with God is very important to him and so he considers everything he does and examines every intention and thought. He is sensitive to the peace of God, and the moment he loses that peace he knows he has sinned. The moment he understands he has sinned, he repents. He does not hide sin that he loves, but always walks in God's light. His relationship with God is the most important thing in his life. Everything else becomes secondary. The commandment *"You shall love the Lord your God with all your heart, with all your soul, and with all your strength"* (Deuteronomy 6:5) is his way of life in every sphere.

4. **He walked with Me in ... equity (integrity).** Many of us bargain with God and try to outwit Him. We try to deceive Him and ourselves in all sorts of ways. We build our influence, our ministry and our importance while pretending to be working for Him. We seek respect from people, publicity, power, influence and money while we are working "for Him" - and we cannot see anything wrong with it. A faithful messenger of the Lord sees these things, confesses them and flees from them. The Lord's messenger walks uprightly with God and does not hide anything from Him. He does not argue and bargain with God but immediately gives everything to Him. He flees from everything that smells of iniquity. His integrity guides his steps and actions.

5. **Turned many away from iniquity.** His purpose is not only that he will flee from sin, but that others around him will also keep away from sin. He points out sin and the way of repentance. He tells people about the Messiah and about God's salvation and in response people repent. People who are not believers come to faith, and those who are believers draw closer to God through his teaching, his works and the testimony of his life.

6. **His lips will keep knowledge.** In order to *keep* knowledge, you first need to *have* knowledge. He reads and studies the Word of God and delves deeply into it. When he sees that people are drifting further from God's truth he is not afraid to tell them so, lovingly and peacefully. When he sees the Church drifting and becoming more like the society around them, contrary to the Word of God, he puts his finger in the dike hole. The knowledge of God is the most important thing to him; this is what he speaks about and this is what he keeps at the center of his life, including his family's life and his church's life. He does not think that he knows and understands everything and is willing to change his viewpoints if he understands from the Scriptures that he is mistaken. He does not try to adapt the Scriptures to his viewpoints, but rather to adapt himself and his surroundings to God's truth.

7. **People will seek the law from his mouth.** All the other points relate to the way the messenger lives out his relationship with God, with the people surrounding him and with how he conducts himself before God. This point speaks of how people around the messenger that also seek God, see him. It is not speaking here of being famous or about his public image, but of the messenger's testimony in his personal and family life. People living around him can come close enough to truly get to know him. It is not only about his image. Furthermore, when they truly get to know him they see and understand that they can learn from him. Again the emphasis is not on his public image but on his personal life. Therefore, he must be transparent to people around him. These

people understand and see that he has something meaningful to say and teach, and that they are able to learn from him. They observe his life and see an example of someone who lives uprightly, in truth and in the peace of God. They see that the knowledge of God and His truth is more important to him than people's opinion of him. They also see that he indeed loves God with all his might, soul and strength. These people will look to him to hear the truth from his mouth.

These are the requirements for the Lord's messenger who serves Him. We must strive for these things and adapt ourselves to them. Is the Holy Spirit showing you things that you must correct? Do you see areas in your life that you must change in order to be a faithful messenger for God?

Day 29

*"**But you have departed from the way; You have caused many to stumble at the law. You have corrupted the covenant of Levi**," says the Lord of hosts. "Therefore I also have made you contemptible and base before all the people, **because you have not kept My ways But have shown partiality in the law**."* (Malachi 2:8-9)

Many times we think that when we do something contrary to God's will we do not affect others. We think that maybe we are hurting ourselves but we are not harming others. However, this verse says that when we turn aside and cease to live our lives fulfilling our duties according to the covenant that God has called us to, it will cause those around us to stumble.

Everything we do, every thought or intention affects not only us but also the people around us. Naturally we cannot be perfect in all our deeds and thoughts – that is not the meaning – that is why the grace of God is given to us to cover for our sins. This is the covenant God made with us. Each time we corrupt the covenant - each time we choose to do something that is against His will, each time we allow pride, unforgiveness or lust into our hearts, and each time we desire to exalt ourselves together with God - we cause not only ourselves to stumble but many others, especially those closest to us.

It is important for us to be aware that we are not an island living independently from others. The things we do, our attitudes and even our thoughts (because they lead to actions) affect the world around us. *"Therefore whatever you have spoken in the dark will be heard in the light, and what you have spoken in the ear in inner rooms will be proclaimed on the housetops."* (Luke 12:3) If we show partiality in the law, i.e. permit things for certain people that we prohibit from others, we cause many to stumble.

Most of us do not realize that this is what we do. We all allow ourselves things that we do not allow others. We allow ourselves liberties while our requirements from others are very high. We understand why we stumble and give ourselves a greater measure of grace than we give others. Either we need to demand of ourselves the same as we demand of others, or we need to require of others only what we require of ourselves. This is how we show partiality in the law. Because of God's grace toward us it is appropriate that we give the same grace to others and only require them to meet the same requirements we demand of ourselves, perhaps even less.

God is a God of covenants. He makes a covenant with those who love and follow Him, and He is always faithful to His covenant. We corrupt His covenant and disgrace it.

Come before Him in prayer and see if you have turned aside from the way, see if you have given yourself allowances that you do not give others, whether your requirements from others are higher than what you require from yourself. See if you have corrupted the covenant of God and have been unfaithful; if you see it in your life - repent.

Day 30

"Have we not all one Father? Has not one God created us? Why do we deal treacherously with one another by profaning the covenant of the fathers?" (Malachi 2:10)

Since the writer speaks of creation and all having one father we understand that the covenant referred to in this verse is the covenant with Noah in Genesis: *"Surely for your lifeblood I will demand a reckoning; from the hand of every beast I will require it, and from the hand of man. From the hand of every man's brother I will require the life of man. Whoever sheds man's blood, by man his blood shall be shed; For in the image of God He made man."* (Genesis 9:5-6)

The first covenant that God made with man states that He has created us, and that we all have one father namely Adam. For this reason, we must treat all people with respect *"For in the image of God He made man."*

Our inclination is to see the world through the spectacles of "us" and "them", our group and theirs. Our family is the one that does things the right way, our church is the right one, our country, our culture, even our favorite sports team. We are better and more righteous, the others are not and therefore are inferior to us.

I have met people who believe in the baptism and gifts of the Holy Spirit, who view with contempt those who do not believe that the gifts of the Spirit are intended for today. I have also met those who do not believe in the gifts of the Spirit, who regard with contempt those who do. "They might be believers, but a little less than us", they say - or at least think.

Many in Israel view the Arabs as inferior. "They are our enemies that only want to kill us. God gave us this land and they pose a threat to us, therefore we need to kill them/expel them/show them who is boss (choose the correct term)."

God created all of us in His image and likeness. He is the Father of us all and He loves those who are different and strangers, just as He loves us, even unto His death on the cross. *"One law shall be for the native-born and for the stranger who dwells among you."* (Exodus 12:49) An important part of the law speaks of protecting the foreigner and the stranger among us. We must see others and those who are different, the Arab and the Gay, the charismatic and the one who is opposed to the gifts of the Spirit through God's eyes. We must treat others the same way He treats us. He loves us even when He does not agree with all the things we do, so we must treat others in the same way.

When we treat others disrespectfully as though they are a lesser creation of God than we are, we profane God's covenant.

How do you relate to those who are different from you? Do different political or theological viewpoints cause you to look down on others?

Day 31

"Have we not all one Father? Has not one God created us? **Why do we deal treacherously with one another** *by profaning the covenant of the fathers?"* (Malachi 2:10)

Dealing treacherously is betrayal. Betrayal is a hurtful thing. There is not one among us who have not experienced it to some degree or another. Someone we trusted, felt close to, or a friend whom we allowed to get to know us better than others – betrayed us. Someone to whom we opened the intimate parts of our heart, who then used what we showed them to advance themselves or to hurt us. We gave our heart, the most precious thing to us, and this person broke it, threw it on the floor and trampled it with their feet.

When we begin to think of betrayal we remember immediately a number of incidents where people have betrayed us and hurt us. Those who betrayed us did not treat us with the measure of respect wherewith we treated them, and they hurt us deeply. Betrayal is one of the most hurtful things and therefore it is difficult for us to forgive those who betray us.

God is the One who has been betrayed the most, and yet continues to love. We are the ones who have betrayed and still betray Him. This is one of the hardest things for us to accept – that we ourselves are betrayers. We regarded others as instruments to be used in order to advance ourselves. We use intimate knowledge about people to advance our causes. We ourselves were unfaithful to those who were closest to us. Perhaps most importantly, we ourselves have betrayed God's covenants and in so doing have hurt Him. We took that which was most precious to God, His beloved Son Jesus the Messiah, our Righteousness; and have disrespected Him and trampled on Him. We ourselves tried to advance ourselves by using Him and steal the glory that is due to Him. It is easy to remember those who have betrayed us, but in reality we are the ones betraying those who are close to us, especially God. As we find it written in 1 Peter 4:17, *"the time has come for judgment to begin at the house of God."* Judgment and repentance must start with us.

When we hurt God He remains faithful and never betrays us. In the same way, we must also love those that betray us. When you pray choose to forgive those who have betrayed you.

Do you have the courage to truly admit that you are a betrayer and repent? A messenger of God must be faithful to the Sender and seek not to betray Him. He must be faithful to his calling and commission and not seek his own good nor to promote himself. Are you willing to admit that you yourself have been/are a betrayer? Prayerfully repent.

Day 32

"Judah has dealt treacherously, and an abomination has been committed in Israel and in Jerusalem, for Judah has profaned the Lord's holy institution which He loves: He has married the daughter of a foreign god. May the Lord cut off from the tents of Jacob the man who does this, being awake and aware, yet who brings an offering to the Lord of hosts!" (Malachi 2:11-12)

After emphasizing the covenant that we made with Him, God moves onto the covenant which is of second importance; the marriage covenant. Every covenant that we make with people, we make it also with their God (or gods). For this reason, God commanded the children of Israel: *"You shall make no covenant with them, nor with their gods."* (Exodus 23:32) That is why it is said in the New Covenant: *"Do not be unequally yoked together with unbelievers. For what fellowship has righteousness with lawlessness? And what communion has light with darkness?"* (2 Corinthians 6:14)

God simply says that when we make covenants with people we become their partners, and partakers in all covenants under whose authority they are. This means that if we marry someone to whom money and power, influence or pleasure is god, or to whom they are their own god; we become partners of their god and so commit idolatry. Of this it is written: *"Can two walk together, unless they are agreed?"* (Amos 3:3)

Part of the covenant that we made with God says, that every covenant we make with other people must fall under the covenant we have with Him. Therefore, marriage, business partnerships or any other covenant that we make must be only with those who themselves have a covenant with God. The moment we become partners with non-believers, we profane the holiness of God and marry a *"daughter of a foreign god."*

There are exceptions when children of those who are married to non-believers continue to walk in the faith, but these are the exceptions not the rule. The result of entering a marriage covenant with a non-believing person is usually that the fruit of the covenant is cut off from the tents of Jacob, and that they no longer belong to those who bring an offering to the Lord of Hosts.

We must not take lightly the covenants we make. They have consequences - blessings if they are made under God's authority or curses if not.

Do you examine whether your covenants and your partnerships are made in the light of the Scriptures? Does the Word of God guide you or is it your own desires and emotions?

Day 33

***"And this is the second thing you do: You cover the altar of the Lord with tears, with weeping and crying; So** (Because) **He does not regard the offering anymore, nor receive it with goodwill from your hands**.*" (Malachi 2:13)

In the midst of reproving their unfaithfulness God reminds the hearers that He is pointing out sin not in order for them to feel guilty, but in order that they may repent. God's people are trying again and again to hide their sin and to argue with God. In His Faithfulness He tries again and again to lead them to repentance seeing that only repentance can bring them back to the right place before God; to make their offerings acceptable.

Even during repentance, we tend to concentrate on ourselves. Repentance is not only crying and shedding tears for moving away from God's blessing or being sorry for sinning and for our imperfection, but it involves crying tears over God's altar. Repentance is crying and shedding tears because we have hurt God, harmed His work and that we are no longer in the center of His will for our lives because we were unfaithful to Him. The crying must be because of the fact that we have hurt and betrayed Him. This crying must be done upon God's altar, at the foot of the cross while accepting the sacrifice that God gave us as atonement for our sin.

Repentance is not just being sorry for my sin, it is not just crying because I am not perfect and I have lost God's blessing; but it involves coming to the cross with crying and groaning over the pain I am causing God with my unfaithfulness and then accepting His forgiveness through the sacrifice that He gave, Jesus the Messiah.

Accepting the forgiveness is an important part of repentance and includes accepting forgiveness from God, and forgiving myself.

Again, God's purpose in reproof is not to lay blame but rather that we may repent and return to the place of faithfulness to Him, a place where our sacrifice is accepted —where we are close to Him, sitting on His lap, resting ourselves on His heart. Only in that place does our service and mission truly serve the One who sent us.

God loves us and wants us to be close to Him; therefore, He hates anything that distances us from Him. This is why He hates sin.

How is your repentance? Does it concentrate on you and the things you did or upon God and the things He has done? Does it concentrate on the pain that your failure causes you or the pain that it causes God?

Day 34

Yet you say, "For what reason?" **Because the Lord has been witness between you and the wife of your youth, with whom you have dealt treacherously; Yet she is your companion and your wife by covenant.** *But did He not make them one, having a remnant of the Spirit? And why one? He seeks godly offspring. Therefore, take heed to your spirit, and let none deal treacherously with the wife of his youth. For the Lord God of Israel says that He hates divorce, for it covers one's garment with violence," Says the Lord of hosts. "Therefore take heed to your spirit, that you do not deal treacherously."* (Malachi 2:14-16)

Here it speaks of a covenant with a woman, but the whole passage speaks of marriage partners and is relevant to both husbands and wives.

In a marriage covenant the marriage partner is a partner in covenant, a friend. The world today emphasizes the individual and his independence. Even in marriage the emphasis is on fulfilling my needs, expectations and desires. A covenant makes the covenant partners one unit. They are no longer two individuals but one flesh. Individuals cannot see the fruit of God in marriage. *Godly offspring,** God's fruit, comes only when the two become one.

---

* In Hebrew literally "God's seed".

Marriage is not the loose association of two individuals for the achievement of a common purpose. Marriage is a covenant in which the two become one and therefore it is highly important that we dedicate much prayer and thought when choosing a partner.

There are people who are in love with the idea of marriage. They think that the moment you marry life begins and all problems are solved. It is not so. The moment you marry the process of making the two individuals into one unit begins. This process is not always pleasant and involves painful changes in the individual, struggles between the partners and struggles of both partners with themselves. Many times when one or both partners are not willing to give up their individuality these struggles cause a distancing between the partners and then they do not become one. If the partners are indeed willing to give up their individuality to become one, they go through the stages of pain and struggle while giving and receiving forgiveness until they enter into a special intimacy – the intimacy intended by God through the unity of covenant. This unity in married life helps us to understand our unity with God and the covenant He made with us.

How do you view your married life? Are you in this relationship to fulfill your needs? Do you view your wife (or your husband) as one with yourself or as someone separate from you? Do you have separate bank accounts or joint ones? Are you willing to give up your individuality to be one with your spouse? Are you willing to suffer pain again and again, and forgive as God forgives you? Only in this way will you enter into the unity and intimacy that God intended for us.

Day 35

Yet you say, "For what reason?" Because the Lord has been witness between you and the wife of your youth, **with whom you have dealt treacherously; Yet she is your companion and your wife by covenant. But did He not make them one, having a remnant of the Spirit? And why one? He seeks godly offspring. Therefore take heed to your spirit, and let none deal treacherously with the wife of his youth.** *"For the Lord God of Israel says that He hates divorce, for it covers one's garment with violence," Says the Lord of hosts.* **"Therefore take heed to your spirit, that you do not deal treacherously.***"* (Malachi 2:14-16)

Women and men are unfaithful in different ways. With men unfaithfulness usually starts with the eyes. Looking at other women's bodies whether in the real world or the virtual world, and by letting the imagination of sexual activity with other women run wild. An imagination let loose to dwell on other women's bodies leads to breaking the marriage covenant, to committing adultery. The door was opened and that is why Jesus said, *"whoever looks at a woman to lust for her has already committed adultery with her in his heart."* (Matthew 5:28)

In women the unfaithfulness starts with emotional dissatisfaction with the husband, and comparing him to other men: "If my husband was a little more spiritual, a bit more considerate, a bit more tender, and like so and so…" This leads to imaginations of how it would have been if I was married to that other person who is more spiritual, considerate and more tender than my husband. Following this, the imagination is let loose to live a married life with a man other than her husband, and this leads to the breaking of the marriage covenant, to committing adultery.

Committing adultery is only the tip of the iceberg; and just like most of the iceberg is invisible to the eye but is even more dangerous than the visible part, so it is with adultery. The real adultery begins when we allow our thoughts and imaginations to dwell whether sexually or emotionally with someone who is not part of our marriage covenant. Therefore, the emphasis in these verses are that if we desire to be faithful we have to take heed in our spirit. We have to stop the unfaithfulness before the unfaithfulness settles in our imagination, takes root and then of course bears fruit.

Faithfulness to the covenant means being faithful at all levels: in practice, in thought and in the emotions.

Unfaithfulness begins in the imagination, in the spirit. Is your imagination clean? Have you allowed your imagination to develop a relationship (sexual or emotional) with someone else who is not part of your marriage covenant? Men, do you allow your eyes to lead you or do you lead your eyes? Women, do you compare your husband to other men? Repent, clean up your imagination and be faithful to the covenant you have made.

Day 36

Yet you say, "For what reason?" Because the Lord has been witness between you and the wife of your youth, with whom you have dealt treacherously; Yet she is your companion and your wife by covenant. But did He not make them one, having a remnant of the Spirit? And why one? He seeks godly offspring. Therefore take heed to your spirit, and let none deal treacherously with the wife of his youth. **"For the Lord God of Israel says that He hates divorce, for it covers one's garment with violence,"** *Says the Lord of hosts. "Therefore take heed to your spirit, that you do not deal treacherously."* (Malachi 2:14-16)

God hates divorce. It does not matter how the world views it, or even how the Church views it – God hates divorce. He hates divorce because it is a violation of a covenant between people, a covenant that reflects His covenant with us, and He does not divorce. Faithfulness is more important to God than the personal satisfaction of the marriage partners.

In the Scriptures God permits divorce for only two reasons: 1. When one of the partners commits adultery.* 2. When one of the partners comes to faith and the other partner (the non-believer) chooses to divorce because of that.† The moment you give

---

* *And I say to you, whoever divorces his wife, except for sexual immorality, and marries another, commits adultery; and whoever marries her who is divorced commits adultery.* (Matthew 19:9).
† *But if the unbeliever departs, let him depart; a brother or a sister is not under bondage in such cases. But God has called us to*

yourself to Jesus there are no other reasons for divorce permitted in the Scriptures.

Society permits divorce for many reasons, such as incompatibility, loss of excitement, loss of love, self-fulfillment and many other reasons that do not fit in with the Scriptures. Unfortunately, many churches and many believers in the Western world accept these as legitimate reasons for divorce. In many countries there is hardly any difference between the rate of divorce among believers than among the rest of society. Instead of requiring society to adapt itself to the standard of the Scriptures, Christians adopt the social standards of society.

Very few people stand against the tide, or stand in the gap and shout: "Sin!" When someone cries out and points out sin, he is rejected while the people block their ears to the truth. God's messenger must live God's truth and declare it even if he goes against the tide, and even if he is rejected because of it.

God hates divorce. There are no two ways about it. The result of breaking the marriage covenant is that instead of clothing ourselves with God's righteousness, the garments of salvation, that the world may see; we are now covered with defilement and that is what is seen. We disgrace God. In my own marriage we even forbade ourselves from mentioning the word divorce when we argued.

---

peace. (1 Corinthians 7:15).

How do you view divorce? Is it at all an option in your marriage? Is it an option in your church? Decide to be faithful to your spouse even under difficult circumstances and in hard times.

Day 37

You have wearied the Lord with your words; *Yet you say, "In what way have we wearied Him?" In that you say, "Everyone who does evil is good in the sight of the Lord, and He delights in them," Or, "Where is the God of justice?"* (Malachi 2:17)

God does not get tired because of Israel's arguments with Him, since *"He who keeps Israel shall neither slumber nor sleep."* (Psalms 121:4) However, He does stop trying to show them that they are mistaken and must change their ways. Instead of correcting them He lets them continue and receive the fruit of their works. We can make God weary with our arguments. Again, it is not that He becomes tired, but that He stops making an effort to convince us that we are wrong and allows us to suffer the consequences of our choices.

No one likes to be shown their own mistakes. When a light shine on those areas that we try to hide, our tendency is to try and justify ourselves and the things we do. We are great experts at coming up with reasons why what we do is okay. Like the children of Israel, we too tend to argue with God and try to convince Him that what we are doing is fine. We turn things we want into things we need, and think we know best what is good for us. The worst thing that happens is that we weary God so much that He stops trying to show us that we are mistaken, and then gives us what we so much desire – the things we "nag" Him for.

We know people who so much wanted to get married that they were not willing to listen to the warnings that God sent them regarding the partner they chose. God allowed them to marry and they suffered the rest of their lives for making that choice. The fact that God stopped trying to dissuade them from marrying that partner did not come about because He finally understood that they were right and He was wrong, but because their arguments wearied Him.

One of the sad verses in the Bible is in Psalm 106:15, this speaks of the children of Israel in the wilderness who asked God for what they thought was good for them, *"And He gave them their request, but sent leanness into their soul."* He gave them what they wanted, but the result was leanness in their soul. In contrast Jesus said, *"not My will, but Yours, be done."* (Luke 22:42) They wanted their will and were not willing to relent; Jesus did not want His will but the Father's. They thought they knew better than God what was good for them. Jesus knew that the Father knew best what was good for Him.

A messenger of God knows that all God's thoughts towards him are good, and that God knows better than he himself what is good for him, because God knows him better that he knows himself.

Do you desire something so badly that you nag God to give it to you? Do you understand that God knows better than you what is good for you? Be careful not to weary God so that He just gives you what you want.

Day 38

"Behold, I send My messenger, and he will prepare the way before Me. *And the Lord, whom you seek, will suddenly come to His temple, even the Messenger of the covenant, in whom you delight. Behold, He is coming," Says the Lord of hosts.* (Malachi 3:1)

God always prepares the way; He never does anything without preparation. *"But when the fullness of the time had come, God sent forth His Son, born of a woman, born under the law."* (Galatians 4:4) Throughout all of history ever since sin in the garden of Eden, God prepared man for the coming of the Messiah, at the right moment He sent His Son. Likewise, today, God is preparing His future works both in the world and in the hearts of men.

God sends His messengers in order to prepare His way. Our role as God's messengers is to clear His path, to prepare the way for Him. We do not know when the fullness of time will come. We cannot make people walk in His way, we do not always know where the path leads and what turns it will have, but our role is to clear the path both in society and in the hearts of men around us. It is important to understand that our role is not to pave His way, set God's direction and tell Him how He should work, nor it is to make people walk in His ways – this is the role of the Holy Spirit. Our role is only to prepare and clear the way.

We know when we speak to people about the Messiah that there are many things preventing them from seeing the truth, such as Christian History riddled with persecution of the Jews, the corruption of the Church and believers, the teachings of the rabbis, "science" that teaches that there is no God, sin that prevents people from submitting to God and numerous other stumbling blocks which prevent people from walking in God's way. Our role which we should execute gently with love and patience, is to try to remove these stumbling blocks in people's lives around us. Again, we cannot force people to walk in God's way, but we *can* remove obstacles from their way and especially not be an obstacle ourselves.

Many times the greatest obstacle for people around us is the hardness of our own hearts, our pride and our behavior. Believers who view themselves as better and more spiritual than people around them are an obstacle for these people to receive the love of the Messiah. Many times the best way to remove obstacles from people's lives around us, is to first let God break our stony hearts and transform us into His image.

Do you allow God to clear the way in your own heart? Do you live your life as a path-clearer in the lives of people around you, or are you trying to make them walk in God's way? Settle that in prayer in the presence of God.

Day 39

"Behold, I send My messenger, and he will prepare the way before Me. **And the Lord, whom you seek, will suddenly come to His temple, even the Messenger of the covenant, in whom you delight. Behold, He is coming**,*" Says the Lord of hosts.* (Malachi 3:1)

This verse is one of the clearest promises about the Messiah and is another stage in preparing the nation for the coming of the promised One. Although this verse is very clear and the Jewish commentators of old understood it quite correctly, the coming of the Messiah still took them by surprise and they rejected Him.

According to Jewish religious commentators, that *messenger* is Elijah, *the Lord* is God and the Messenger of the Covenant is the high priest/ Elijah/ the Messiah. Rashi (a famous Jewish commentator) on Malachi 3:1 says, "*the Lord* is the *God of justice*." Rabbi Meïr Leibush ben Yehiel, Michel Wisser (known as Malbim), who lived in the 19th century writes regarding this, "Then the Lord will come to dwell in His lower sanctuary [that is, the earthly one] and walk in the midst of them." In the "Metzudat David", which was written by Rabbi David Altschuler and his son Rabbi Yehiel Hillel in the 17th century, it says regarding Malachi 3:1, "*Behold, He is coming*" it is written in the past tense [Futuristic Past tense in Hebrew I.H.] for when Messiah comes, Elijah will have already come for he will precede him, "*in whom you delight"* – [means] that he will come to proclaim redemption and raise the dead. His future intention is to proclaim [both] that and the resurrection, as it is written at the end of the book, *"Behold, I will send you Elijah the prophet"* etc.; and *"the Messenger of the covenant"* – he will be called Elijah the prophet for he was jealous for the covenant of circumcision which prevented the kingdom of Ephraim, and so [say] our rabbis, blessed be their memory; *the Lord* etc. - this is the King Messiah for which every eye is looking in expectation and hope and asking for his coming."

In the New Covenant we see reference to the fact that the messenger sent to clear the way is indeed in some way Elijah the prophet, and the fulfillment is in John the Baptist.

Despite all their understanding of the Scriptures when John came to clear the way of the Lord, and God came and dwelt in His sanctuary in Messiah Jesus, He was not accepted and they turned against Him.

It is easy for us to point a finger at them and wonder how they could not see and did not understand, but we also have difficulty in understanding God's time and the way in which He works. Even when He prepares the way and always acts in the fullness of time, when He acts, we are surprised. How many times do we pray that something will happen and then we are surprised when God answers?

God's messenger always needs to be aware of his pride. Pride that manifests itself in the thought that he is better than those that do not believe. Pride that manifests itself in the thought that we know how God works, and what He intends to do. Do you think you know exactly how things will happen in the future? And what will happen when Messiah returns? Will there be a rapture of the saints before the great tribulation? After the great tribulation? In the middle of the great tribulation? Beware! The Pharisees also thought they know exactly when the Messiah will come, and when He did not come in the way they thought He would they did not recognize Him. It is important to know the prophecies and to study them, but we should not think that we know exactly how God will work. We should not presume to fully understand God's ways and plans. God's messenger works in humility and meekness, and he knows his limitations.

Do you presume you fully understand God's ways and thoughts? Do you think you know His exact future steps? Beware and repent.

Day 40

"Behold, I send My messenger, and he will prepare the way before Me. **And the Lord, whom you seek, will suddenly come to His temple, even the Messenger of the covenant, in whom you delight** *(Hebrew – hafetzin/Desire).* **Behold, He is coming**,*" Says the Lord of hosts.* (Malachi 3:1)

This declaration is amazing. The Lord will come to His temple; the Messenger of the covenant will come soon. This is not something that is written in the New Covenant, but in the Old. The declaration is so amazing that the nation of Israel is not willing to accept it, therefore, when it suddenly happened it surprised them.

The Lord, a term understood even by the rabbis as speaking of God, will come to His temple. What is written here is that God Himself will come to the temple and that God Himself is the Messenger of the covenant. There is a parallelism in this verse between *the Lord* and *the Messenger of the covenant*, and between *whom you seek* and *in whom you desire*.

After God reproves the people for breaking the various covenants, He says that the One to fix the situation is He Himself, who will come as the Messenger of the covenant. We know that this indeed was fulfilled in Jesus the Messiah a few hundred years after this promise. The Messenger of the covenant, God Himself, came in the Messiah and made a New Covenant with us, so that all would know Him from the smallest to the greatest (Jeremiah 31:31-34).

God sends His messenger to prepare the way, but He Himself comes to His temple to mend the relationship, the covenant.

We too who were called to clear the obstacles need to understand that although our calling indeed is to point to and clear the obstacles from God's way, yet He is the One who will enter the sanctuary and He is the One who will mend hearts. We cannot save people. We cannot change their hearts, bring them into covenant with God or fix their lives – only God can do that.

Many times we try to do things in people's lives that only God can do. We try to force them to enter into covenant with God, we try to fix their lives and change their hearts. It is interesting that many times we think we know exactly what God wants for other people and what His plans are for them, while it is much harder for us to know His plan for ourselves. Humility understands that if it is hard for me to know God's plan for my own life, then perhaps the plan that I see so clearly for others is not really from God but from me? God's messenger needs to have the humility that understands not only what he is able and called to do, but also what he is not able to do. We do indeed need to clear His way, but then we must have patience and humility and let Him come and work in His own way and time.

Day 41

"Behold, I send My messenger, and he will prepare the way before Me. And the Lord, whom you seek, will suddenly come to His temple, even the Messenger of the covenant, in whom you delight. Behold, He is coming," Says the Lord of hosts. **"But who can endure the day of His coming? And who can stand when He appears? For He is like a refiner's fire and like launderers' soap."** (Malachi 3:1-2)

Everybody is waiting for the Messiah. Almost everyone says they wish the Messiah would come, solve all the problems and bring peace to the world. Along many of the roads in Israel there are posters that declare, "We want Messiah now". These posters express the desire in the hearts of people throughout the world not only of the people in Israel.

In these verses God recognizes the people's request and He knows their desires, but because He knows what will really happen He warns them that the coming of the Messiah will not be as they expect. They expect peace and tranquility but the Messiah will be like a refiner's fire. They hope that when Messiah comes their struggles will cease but instead of that He will be like a launderer's soap that reaches deep into the heart to cleanse it.

Notice the different emphasis that distinguishes between God and man. They think Messiah will leave them in peace - since that they are not the problem -

to take care of the "real" problems in the world. God thinks the world's problems begin in the hearts of people and in their personal lives. God knows that in order to solve the problems of the world the individual's life and heart needs to be purified and cleansed first. When we run into a difficulty or a problem do we pray and expect God to solve it by changing others who caused us these difficulties?

Do you also think that the source of your troubles and problems in life are other people and not yourself?

God thinks that in order to solve the problems around you He must begin with you. Are you allowing Him to do that or are you trying to turn God's spotlight away from your problems, to the problems of others? Are you trying to avoid having to go through the painful purifying fire and the soap that rubs and hurts?

In order to be faithful messengers we must understand that the source of our problems begin with us, and allow Him to start the work of purification and cleansing in our hearts. Also, as part of clearing the way of the Lord our work involves explaining to people around us that fixing the world must begin with the fixing of their own hearts, which comes through repentance. We must direct them to God and ask Him to clean and purify them. Do you allow God to refine you?

Day 42

"Behold, I send My messenger, and he will prepare the way before Me. And the Lord, whom you seek, will suddenly come to His temple, even the Messenger of the covenant, in whom you delight. Behold, He is coming," Says the Lord of hosts. "But who can endure the day of His coming? And who can stand when He appears? **For He is like a refiner's fire and like launderers' soap. He will sit as a refiner and a purifier of silver; He will purify the sons of Levi, and purge them as gold and silver, that they may offer to the Lord an offering in righteousness.** *Then the offering of Judah and Jerusalem will be pleasant to the Lord, as in the days of old, as in former years."* (Malachi 3:1-4)

The Messenger of the covenant, the Lord who visits His temple, did not come to make it all nice and pleasant for us – He came to purify the sons of Levi. He came to put our hearts and thoughts through the fire, through the furnace so that the dross will rise to the surface to enable Him to remove it. The purpose of His fire is not to cause pain (although it does bring pain) but to purify. The purpose of the soap is not to point out dirt but rather to clean.

Although we very quickly see dirt in others, we try hard not to see the dirt that is inside ourselves. Our natural inclination is to run away. We run away from difficulties, complain about the fire and we hide the dirt - because the purifying fire hurts. It is important that we understand this fact; the purpose of the burning is not to hurt, but to purify so that we may bring offerings through His righteousness and not our own.

God's messenger has to be one who seeks the fire, and who seeks this cleansing while resisting his natural inclinations to hide and run away, seeing that his whole purpose is to offer a pure offering unto God in His righteousness. Jesus referred to this when he said, *'If anyone desires to come after Me, let him deny himself, and take up his cross, and follow Me."* (Matthew 16:24-28). Jesus, the Messenger of the covenant showed us the way when He chose *"not My will, but Yours, be done."* (Luke 22:42). He chose to suffer, and He chose to go to the cross. It was He who said, *"I came to send fire on the earth, and how I wish it were already kindled!"* (Luke 12:49)

How do you react when God points out sin in your life? Do you try to hide it and justify yourself or do you see it as part of the purifying process to receive His righteousness, and thank Him for it? Do you thank God for the difficulties in your life and say together with Jesus, *"not My will, but Yours, be done?"*

When you present God's way to people do you present it as an easy and pleasant way, or as a way by which the Lord and the Messenger of the covenant refines us with fire and cleanses the dirt in our lives? Do you present God's way faithfully or do your try to beautify it?

Day 43

"And I will come near you for judgment; I will be a swift witness against sorcerers, against adulterers, against perjurers, against those who exploit wage earners and widows and orphans, and against those who turn away an alien— Because they do not fear Me," *Says the Lord of hosts.* (Malachi 3:5)

God warns the people very clearly that He will judge them; in this judgment He is both the judge and the witness. The warning is given to cause them to think before they act in order to instill the fear of God in their hearts.

God does not judge from a distance without knowing each case in-depth. He is near to everyone, He knows everyone better then they know themselves, and He sees all their circumstances. This is one of the reasons why Jesus came to earth and was tempted in every sin just as we are, so that no one can tell the Judge of all the earth, "You have no idea what I am going through."

God is also a witness. He does not only see the things that we do, but also the thoughts and attitudes of our heart, and therefore not only our deeds will be judged but also our will, our thoughts, our imaginations and our motives. He sees them and understands them better than we do.

He is a *swift witness*. He is quick to testify against the sorcerers, the adulterers, the liars, those who exploit workers, those who hurt the poor, the weak and the stranger. He is quick to testify against those who do not fear Him. Judgment against these people come quickly, even if in our understanding it might seem as though it takes a long time. These people receive the fruit of their works during their lifetime.

Sorcery or witchcraft is manipulation of others by unfair means. That is to say, when we try to cause people to do our will - not by asking them directly, but rather "change (them)...by unfair means as to serve one's purpose"*. These unfair means can be an indirect influence without their knowledge, or applying indirect pressure, whether it is mental, social or spiritual to make them do what we want.

Adultery is having sexual relations with someone who is not my husband or wife, whether in practice or in the imagination.

Perjurers are those who treat something false as though it were true, or something true as if it were false.

Those who exploit wage earners are those who do not give what is due to those who work or act on their behalf. An example of this apart from the financial aspect is, when someone helps me to do something

---

* http://www.merriam-webster.com/dictionary/manipulate

and I take all the credit without giving them the credit that is due to them.

Exploiting the weak is damaging or hurting anyone who is weaker than myself, in order to make me feel stronger and better, advancing my cause at their cost.

God is near. He sees every deed, every thought, every desire and every motive. He is both the witness and the judge, and He warns us in advance that we will be judged so that we may live in the fear of God. He warns us so that we will consider everything we do, and every thought we have before we do them. He warns us so that we may live every moment according to His light, and be messengers who live out His message.

As it is written: *"For the word of God is living and powerful, and sharper than any two-edged sword, piercing even to the division of soul and spirit, and of joints and marrow, and is a discerner of the thoughts and intents of the heart.* (Hebrews 4:12) *Therefore be careful how you walk.* (Ephesians 5:15, NASB) *Purify your hearts, you double-minded.* (James 4:8) *Since you have purified your souls in obeying the truth through the Spirit in sincere love of the brethren, love one another fervently with a pure heart."* (1 Peter 1:22)

God's messenger reads the Word of God regularly, studies it and knows it. God's messenger allows the Scriptures to shine into all the dark corners of his heart and thoughts. God's messenger obeys the Scriptures and learns to live by them. He does not manipulate, does not commit adultery, does not bear false testimony, and does not exaggerate when describing things. He gives others what is due to them and protects the weak. Does this describe you?

Day 44

"For I am the Lord, I do not change; Therefore you are not consumed, O sons of Jacob." (Malachi 3:6)

More and more people throughout the world believe that God has changed His choice. According to their view, after God told the people of Israel that He will never leave them, and as long as the sun keeps shining by day and the moon by night that they will continue to be a nation before Him (Jeremiah 31:35-37) They believe that Israel's subsequent national sin caused God to change His mind, to cancel His election of the nation of Israel, and to replace Israel with the world-wide Church. According to this belief Israel no longer has any part in the plan of God, and in His blessing because they have sinned too much; instead, the followers of Jesus are now the true Israel.

Their belief damages their own relationship with God, because if God is not faithful to His promises to the people of Israel, how can He be faithful to His promises to them? Such a belief undermines any confidence in God's faithfulness.

Today's verse clearly contradicts their belief. After God reproves Israel time and again for their sins, He tells them, "I do not change - and because of this, I have not wiped you out." Let us remember that Malachi prophesied after Israel's return to Zion following years of exile, and that Malachi was the last prophet before the coming of Jesus. During this time the question whether God would be fed up with Israel as a nation because of their sins was relevant, and therefore God is very clear here. He tells the people that He is faithful to His promises not because they are not sinning, but because He is God and does not change. The way we regard the nation of Israel in their sin, serves as a testing stone for our own ability to trust that God is also faithful to us in our sin.

Before Moses' death, God gave him what is called "The Song of Moses" (Deuteronomy 32), as a testimony in which God tells the people of Israel what will happen in the future. Israel will sin, God will punish them and afterward bring them back to Himself. In Deuteronomy 31:21 we read, *"Then it shall be, when many evils and troubles have come upon them, that this song will testify against them as a witness; for it will not be forgotten in the mouths of their descendants, for I know the inclination of their behavior today, even before I have brought them to the land of which I swore to give them."* God tells the nation that this song is a testimony to the fact that He knows they will sin. It is no surprise to Him. Nevertheless, He brings them into the land of promise. He knows our tendency to sin, past, present and future, yet remains faithful to us at all times. It is us who think that our sins surprise God and causes Him to give up on us.

God is faithful. If He promises – He fulfills. It is the main part of His character. God's messenger has to be confident that the One sending him is faithful to

His promises regardless of the messenger's faithfulness, because we as messengers fail time and again at presenting a clear message of who God is. In our failures and unfaithfulness and because of them, we have to be confident that the One sending us is faithful even when we fail. Our message is not about our perfection, but about His faithfulness.

Are you confident in God's faithfulness to you? Do you know that He will never leave you? Do you share the message of God's faithfulness?

How do you view the nation of Israel, and what do you teach about the nation of Israel? It is important that the message which the messenger carries will be the message of God's faithfulness even in our imperfection.

Day 45

***"Yet from the days of your fathers you have gone away from My ordinances and have not kept them. Return to Me, and I will return to you," Says the Lord of hosts. "But you said, 'In what way shall we return?'** Do Not Rob God. Will a man rob God? Yet you have robbed Me! But you say, 'In what way have we robbed You?' In tithes and offerings. You are cursed with a curse, for you have robbed Me, even this whole nation."* (Malachi 3:7-9)

Instead of viewing God's declaration of faithfulness to them as a declaration of love, they view it as a weakness. Instead of it causing them to reciprocate with faithfulness they think that God promising not to consume them gives them leverage to bargain with Him, and to gain more things from Him in return for following Him.

'In what way shall we return?' they ask, 'What will you give us if we return?' You do not bargain with God, not just because He is God, but also and perhaps especially, because He already gave everything. *"For God so loved the world that He gave His only begotten Son."* (John 3:16) God answers them very simply, "If you return to Me, you will have Me. *Return to Me, and I will return to you."* For them having God is not enough. They do not want God; they want God's blessings. They do not want Him to control their lives but they want the blessing that comes to those who allow Him control their lives.

The bargaining here is, "What is the least we can give You in order for us to get Your blessing?" They are trying to determine what they will give to God and what they will not. By doing this they are actually telling God, "I will let you be Lord here, but not there; this area in my life is Yours, and that area is not." Not giving over absolute control to God removes God's blessings from them, and places them under the curse.

When we tell God where He can be Lord and where He cannot, we are the real lord of our lives, not Him.

Many people today seek the blessings instead of the Giver of blessings, and the miracles instead of the source of the miracles. It is written that signs and wonders will follow the believers (Mark 16:17), and not that the believers will follow signs and wonders. Let us not seek the blessings, but the One who gives them. God wants to have us in close intimacy with Him. He died on the cross to bring us to Himself and to have an intimate relationship with us, not for our gifts or abilities.

The only reason we should come to God is to have intimacy with Him in return. It is true that His blessings are attractive, but they should not be our motive. Our motive should be our love for Him and our desire to be intimate with Him.
He gave everything. Have you given everything? Do you seek God in order to be close to Him or in order to receive His blessing? Is the message you convey

to others a message of having intimacy with God, or a message about receiving His blessings?

Day 46

"Bring all the tithes into the storehouse, that there may be food in My house, and try Me now in this," *Says the Lord of hosts, "If I will not open for you the windows of heaven and pour out for you such blessing that there will not be room enough to receive it. And I will rebuke the devourer for your sakes, so that he will not destroy the fruit of your ground, nor shall the vine fail to bear fruit for you in the field," Says the Lord of hosts; "And all nations will call you blessed, for you will be a delightful land," Says the Lord of hosts.* (Malachi 3:10-12)

The way you think of your money shows just how much God is the Lord of your life.

Stop and think for a moment: do you think the money you have is yours? Are you the one who determines how much you contribute or give to others? The way you regard money sheds light on the way you regard God. Although God speaks here of giving tithes and offerings, yet if my whole life belongs to Him then all my money belongs to Him too, and He has the right to ask that I give everything. The very struggle such a thought arouses in us shows our difficulty in giving everything to God.

God promises after giving everything including our money to Him, that He will bless us. *"Try Me now in this"*, He says - but we are afraid because if we give everything and He does not bless us then we will be left with nothing. We think that it is best to leave a little bit on the side in case God does not bless us. It is not only in the area of finance, but in every area of our lives that we think it is best to maintain a little bit of control in our own hands, just in case God does not bless us or will not fulfill His promises towards us. This is how Ananias and Sapphira thought in Acts chapter 5, and the consequence was death.

The blessing comes after giving everything to God, not a part, and not almost everything. When we give everything to God, He is the One who protects us from damages and destroyers that want to damage His fruits in our life. When we give everything to God people around us see the blessing, and want to be around us.

Giving the tithe to the church, into the storehouse so that there may be food in His house, is not always easy. We then feel that we lose control of our money and how it will be used. But this serves as a declaration of confidence in God that He is the One who takes care of us, and that we and everything that belongs to us first belonged to Him. Everything without reservation and knowing that it is not up to us to determine where to give, and how it will be used.

How do you see your money? Is it your money? Do you tithe to the church? Do you give more than a tithe?

Day 47

"Bring all the tithes into the storehouse, that there may be food in My house." (Malachi 3:10)

When God tells us to bring tithes and offerings, He tells us to bring it to the storehouse to be used in His house. He is not speaking here about offerings to the poor and needy that should be over and above tithes.

Today there is a tendency amongst believers to think that a church is not something we need to be a part of. "The church is imperfect and defective; therefore, I will not be part of a local church. My believing friends will be my spiritual fellowship, my church", they claim. I have heard of, and spoken to people for whom a religious program on television, Facebook and the internet replaces the local church. It is easier than being part of a local church, as that requires effort. In the local church you need to be involved with sinful and hurting people. In the church the pastor sets the tone, and he is also prone to sin, and not always right. It is true that the television screen protects you against being hurt, and that when you sit in front of the screen no one makes decisions for you, but there is no personal relationship with other people, so your growth is hampered. After all, did not God save us to have intimate relationship with Him and with others? We were created to be in intimate relationships, and this is what we seek throughout our lives.

When we came to faith God added us to a family. Psalm 68:7, "*God sets the solitary in families; ... But the rebellious dwell in a dry land."* He places those who are lonely in homes and in families. With God there is no such thing as a solitary believer. Everyone needs to be part of a home, a family. The local church is a home for the believers, and in the church as it is in a family, the relationships are not always easy but they are necessary and irrevocable. It is impossible not to be part of a family. It is possible to be out of touch with my family but then I am lacking. It could be that I left my family and home and became part of another family (like a foster family), but a person who is in the faith is not alone – he is always part of a family. A person who rejects his family, his home, and who refuses to be part of it is rebellious and dwells in a dry and arid place.

"...not forsaking the assembling of ourselves together, as is the manner of some..." (Hebrews 10:25). God's messenger does not forsake the gathering of the church. God's messenger is part of a church family and is under authority. In the storehouse he is not the one who determines how his tithe will be used.

Running away from being under authority and being part of a congregation harms the messenger, his mission and the message we are called to deliver. Are you part of a local church? Do you view the church as a place where you come to give or as a place where you come to receive? As messengers of God we must give ourselves as He gave Himself.

Day 48

"Your words have been harsh against Me," Says the Lord, "Yet you say, 'What have we spoken against You?' **You have said, 'It is useless to serve God; what profit is it that we have kept His ordinance, and that we have walked as mourners before the Lord of hosts? So now we call the proud blessed, for those who do wickedness are raised up; They even tempt God and go free.'"** *Then those who feared the Lord spoke to one another, and the Lord listened and heard them; So a book of remembrance was written before Him for those who fear the Lord and who meditate on His name.* (Malachi 3:13-16)

As we see here, avoiding to take responsibility for our sin points to deeper problems. Once again God's servants argue with Him when He reproves them. Avoiding to take responsibility originates from their seeing their service to God as something that does not profit them. They compare themselves to others and think others have it easier. "We are serving Him in vain," they say, "What do we gain from the fact that we keep His laws and pull a long and holy face? See what happens to bad people? They are happy and get rich and enjoy themselves while transgressing God's laws and nothing happens to them. Compared to them, our lives are sad and hard and we do not get any reward, so why should we exert ourselves?!"

Comparing our lives to the lives of people around us, shows that we have a problem. King David wrote, "*Do not fret because of evildoers, nor be envious of the workers of iniquity."* (Psalm 37:1) On the surface the lives of those around us, believers and non-believers seem pleasant and easy. It seems to us that we are the only ones having difficulties, and that others around us do not have the same difficulties we struggle with. In fact, the lives of many of those who do not believe seem much easier and more pleasant than those of the believers. They do not battle with sin; they enjoy sinning without guilt. They give account to no one, while we always consider how God and others view what we do.

People who think this way have forgotten what it is like to be without God. They have forgotten the loneliness, the struggle to fit in with society, the desire to be like everyone else, the masks, the guilty feelings, the feeling that no one understands me and accepts me as I truly am nor the efforts to conceal my true self from people.

When you dig a little bit into people's lives whether they are believers or non-believers, you see that it is not easy for anyone, and that people do reap the fruit of their works. To see this just take a look at divorce statistics.

The big difference between believers and non-believers is above all God's grace that covers and forgives, and secondly that we are not alone in our struggle. The God who promised, *"I will never leave you nor forsake you,"* is always with us; He knows us better than we know ourselves and loves us as we are. We have no need to be *walking as mourners*; on the contrary we have many reasons to rejoice. This is the main part of our message: that we are not perfect or better than others, but that God is always with us, and always loves us even unto His death on the cross. His involvement is even into the smallest of detail. He also corrects and improves us. This is love. This is the great difference between us and those who do not believe. This is the good news that we are called to preach. We have received infinite love, and even then we still look for it in all the wrong places.

Day 49

"Your words have been harsh against Me," Says the Lord, "Yet you say, 'What have we spoken against You?' You have said, 'It is useless to serve God; what profit is it that we have kept His ordinance, and that we have walked as mourners before the Lord of hosts? So now we call the proud blessed, for those who do wickedness are raised up; They even tempt God and go free.'" **Then those who feared the Lord spoke to one another, and the Lord listened and heard them; So a book of remembrance was written before Him for those who fear the Lord and who meditate on His name. "They shall be Mine," says the Lord of hosts, "On the day that I make them My jewels.** *And I will spare them as a man spares his own son who serves him."* (Malachi 3:13-17)

Our words have the power to build up or to tear down not only to those around us, but ourselves too. Have you noticed that people who always complain are unhappy people? They do not complain because they are unhappy, they are unhappy because they complain. People who are full of thanksgiving are happier people. They are not full of thanksgiving because they are happy, they are happy because they are full of thanksgiving.

God listens to everything we say, therefore it is important that we think before we speak. The things we say and the way we say them bear fruit.

Those who fear the Lord speak to one another. Those who fear the Lord look for others who fear the Lord to be in touch with them and speak with them. Speaking with one another necessitates fellowship with one another, and when two or three of those who fear the Lord are together – He is with them. Those who fear the Lord are not alone, they are together with others like themselves and their favorite subject of conversation is God and His works. They talk about Him because they think about Him.

The one who loves never ceases to speak well about their beloved. One who fears the Lord does not stop speaking well of the Lord, neither does he speak under compulsion in order to fulfill an obligation. He speaks about God because, *'out of the abundance of the heart the mouth speaks."* (Matthew 12:34).

Speaking and expressing yourself is not only through words, but also through the things you do and the way you live. If the way you live and the things you do, do not express God's character and will, it shows that your heart is full of something or someone else. King David said, *"I will bless the Lord at all times; His praise shall continually be in my mouth."* (Psalms 34:1).

God listens to what we express with our words, but He pays special attention to the things we do, as our actions speak louder than words. He hears the murmurings of our hearts and is aware of our motivations in every matter. He has compassion towards us because of this and He also fully understands us. He prepares those whose heart is upright before Him to be His treasure.

God's messengers are to listen, just as God listens. A faithful messenger of God needs to learn to listen. Listening to the words and the works of those around us will help us to understand them and to communicate with them heart to heart in the fear of the Lord, so that we can help them to grow into God's character.

Someone once said that God gave us two ears and one mouth because He wants us to listen twice as much as we speak. One of the marks of a messenger is that he truly knows how to listen to people around him, and that he tries to understand what is really in their heart.

Do your words and actions carry the same message? Is the message that you convey a message that magnifies God?

Do you know and are learning how to listen? Ask God to help you to listen to people around you, just as He listens to you.

Day 50

"Then you shall again discern between the righteous and the wicked, between one who serves God and one who does not serve Him." (Malachi 3:18)

When God judges the world, we will see who is righteous and who is wicked. All the masks will be removed and we will see the truth about people. What this verse really says is; at this moment we do not see who is really righteous and who is really wicked, who really serves God and who does not.

Most, if not all of us are quick to judge and to determine which person is righteous and which person is not. It is true that when a man murders or rape it is pretty clear that he is wicked and not serving God, but for the most part the situation is not so clear. However, we are quick to judge people and label them as good or bad. We are quick to place people into pigeon holes.

We only see what is on the surface for brief periods. God who sees the depths of the heart at all times, tells Samuel, when He sends him to anoint a king from the sons of Jesse, *"for man looks at the outward appearance, but the Lord looks at the heart."* (1 Samuel 16:7)

As God's messengers we must also understand and accept our own limitations and one of these limitations is, that we do not know everything.

Our tendency to judge people and label them actually harms our mission. Our desire to tag people hinders our ability to love them and to help them grow and develop in God's will. Tagging people places them in a box, and this prevents us from helping them to develop.

I think most, if not all of us were hurt in the past when people judged us, tagged us wrongly and treated us in a certain way despite the fact that we did not deserve that kind of behavior.

As God's messengers we must love people, whether they are righteous or wicked. As God's messengers we must treat people with love while striving to see them grow, develop and draw nearer to the Lord. Such an attitude is only possible if we learn to listen to them, and not predetermine our opinion of them. As God's messengers we must not have preconceived opinions about people, but rather let them and the things they do show us who they are. Even then we must remain open to the fact that we do not see the whole truth.

Do you make up your opinion of people quickly? Do you tag people as good or bad, spiritual or unspiritual without having enough time to get to know them in depth? We must remember that we do not always discern clearly between the righteous and the wicked, between one who serves God and one who does not.

Ask God to give you patience and wisdom to really listen to people around you, and not to put them into boxes.

Day 51

"For behold, the day is coming, burning like an oven, and all the proud, yes, all who do wickedly will be stubble. And the day which is coming shall burn them up," Says the Lord of hosts, "That will leave them neither root nor branch. But to you who fear My name the Sun of Righteousness shall arise with healing in His wings; And you shall go out and grow fat like stall-fed calves." (Malachi 4:1-2)

An important part of our message is that the day of judgment will come, all that is hidden will be revealed, and everything that was done will be tested by the One who sees the heart (1 Samuel 16:7) and does not judge by the sight of His eyes (Isaiah 11:3). There is not one who will not stand in judgment. During Noah's time, judgment came by water, and we are told that the next judgment will be by fire.

Illustrating the use of the sun portrays the correct picture, as the sun both burns and gives life.

In the same way, the fire of God's judgment burns all the proud and evil doers without leaving them a root or a branch. There is no chance that they will be restored to life. Yet, for those who fear His name, that fire, like the sun, gives righteousness and healing, increase and growth. What makes the difference is what is in the hearts of people before judgment comes.

God is as the sun and when He comes near for judgment, He will either burn or give life. On that judgment day a person who fears God and who accepted His authority, and the sacrifice of Messiah, the person who comes to God before God comes to Him for judgment has already been refined with the purifying fire. All the flammable material and all the wickedness has been tried and purified. Their righteousness will be seen, hurts will be healed, and his needs will be met with riches.

Jesus says in Luke 12:49, "*I came to send fire on the earth, and how I wish it were already kindled!*" He is not speaking here only of burning, but also of refining. Jesus does not desire to send His judgment fire, but rather His refining fire. "*God our Savior, who desires all men to be saved and to come to the knowledge of the truth*" (1 Timothy 2:3-4). God desires all men to be saved, and this is why He first sent the Messiah to bring the refining fire to those who received Him. Only after that will He send the burning fire by which everything will be made clear.

On that day, if there is a lot of burning material in the person, he will be consumed, but if the burning material has already been purified, the gold and silver of his works will be made clear, as is written in 1 Corinthians 3:12-13 "*Now if anyone builds on this foundation with gold, silver, precious stones, wood, hay, straw, each one's work will become clear; for the Day will declare it, because it will be revealed by fire; and the fire will test each one's work, of what sort it is.*"

A person who takes upon himself the yoke of the Messiah brings his heart daily to the sun of judgment, into the light of the Scriptures and the Holy Spirit, so that God can try his heart in order to cleanse him from dirt, and this leads him deeper into intimacy with God.

This is our message and this is how we must live our lives. Do we too, like Jesus, desire the refining fire to burn in our lives and refine us? Do we convey to people around us the message of the fire that is coming, and that God in His love and His grace wants to refine us today so that the fire will not consume us?

Day 52

"You shall trample the wicked, for they shall be ashes under the soles of your feet on the day that I do this," Says the Lord of hosts. (Malachi 4:3)

Most of us would have preferred to see the victory of the Messiah over the wicked as soon as possible. We would like to see God judge our enemies, crush them and place them as ashes under our feet. In almost every situation it is pretty clear to us who the wicked one is (the one who is hurting us) and who the righteous one is (us), and we would like for the one who hurts us or whoever we think hurt us, to be under our feet. It is important to us not only to be right, but also that everyone will see that we are right. Therefore, we often take steps to try and place our opponents under our feet. We make ourselves both the judiciary and the executive branch, both judge and executioner.

One of the things God tells us is: not to be quick to judge who is righteous and who is wicked. In the end when everything comes to light, perhaps we will turn out to be those that are wicked.

God says, only in the day that He chooses will we understand who is righteous and who is wicked, who served God and who did not. He is the only one who will cause the wicked to be under the feet of the righteous. Neither will it be today or tomorrow, but in the day that He chooses. We will not place our opponents under our feet, but He will.

In our pride we always believe that we are the ones who are right. We fight to prove that and that the others are wrong. God tells us to let go of our desire for revenge, *"Vengeance is Mine, I will repay," says the Lord."* (Romans 12:19, quoting Deuteronomy 32:35).

In that day everything will come to light, true justice will be done and we will again see who is righteous and who is wicked. I feel that in more cases than we would have liked, we will be the ones found to be wicked. We are not only called to be patient, but also to have a soft heart in constant repentance. A heart that seeks God's kingdom and His righteousness, not our own kingdom and our righteousness. Humility is the hallmark of God's messengers.

One of the slogans used in the campaign against road accidents is, "On the road, don't be right, be wise." I would like to change it a little to, "In life, don't be right, be wise." Do not live with the desire to be right, live with the desire to become wiser.

Is it important for you to be right, and for people around you to know it? Do you take into account that perhaps you are the one who is not correct? Strive to live in a state of constant repentance, so that you do not find yourself in a place where your righteousness is actually a filthy rag in God's sight. *"But we are all like an unclean thing, and all our righteousness are like filthy rags; We all fade as a leaf, and our iniquities, like the wind, have taken us away."* (Isaiah 64:6)

Day 53

"Remember the Law of Moses, My servant, *which I commanded him in Horeb for all Israel, with the statutes and judgments.* ***Behold, I will send you Elijah the prophet before the coming of the great and dreadful day of the Lord.*** *And he will turn the hearts of the fathers to the children, and the hearts of the children to their fathers, lest I come and strike the earth with a curse."* (Malachi 4:4-6)

These well-known verses not only conclude the book, but are the last verses to be written in the Old Covenant. Both of these people, Moses and Elijah appear again in the New Covenant on the mountain (Matthew 17) and point to Jesus as Messiah. These two people bridge the time lapsed (about 400 years), between these verses and the New Covenant.

Moses and Elijah are two messengers of God. One redeemed Israel from bondage in Egypt and brought Israel into the Sinai covenant, and the other is the prophet that stood up against kings, who brought fire down from heaven, brought back a whole nation to worship God, and ascended in a fiery flame into the heavens. Moses and Elijah are both messengers of God, the one called a servant and the other called a prophet. They give closure to the book of Malachi that speaks of God and His messengers, and paved the way for the perfect Messenger, Jesus the Messiah.

God, who of course knew that these are the last verses of the Old Covenant emphasizes two important things here; Do not forget the past *(Remember the Law of Moses)*, and look forward to the future *(Behold, I will send you Elijah the prophet before the coming of the great and dreadful day of the Lord)*. This tension between remembering the past and looking towards the future will keep you in the present. This balance between past and future should not be taken for granted.

The kingdom of heaven is in the present, and therefore the devil will do everything to divert our attention from the present to the past or to the future. Pointing to the Torah and the traditions of the past, or to the prophecies of the future.

He causes us to look backward by convincing us that the past was better, and that we should attempt to live like people lived in the past. A good example of that is the clothing of the Ultra-Orthodox Hassidim Jews, they try to dress in the same style that their rabbi dressed hundreds of years ago, because that is considered spiritual clothing. Or take the Amish community that forbids their members to use modern technology. Another way in which he causes us to remain in the past is, when we do not forgive those who had hurt us, and so causing us to relive the hurts again and again.

In regard to the future, Satan causes us to look into the future by over occupying ourselves with prophecies and their fulfillment, and by getting prepared for the next great disaster that is just around the corner or for the Zombies' War.

Either way we are not living in the present, and the kingdom of God does not get to touch the people present around us.

In the Old Covenant the present is called 'today'. *"Today, if you will hear His voice: Do not harden your hearts"* (Psalm 95:7-8). This means that now we should not harden our hearts. God lives through us in the world now. The past has already happened, the future not yet. Only in the present we can change the world. Only in the present we can touch people's lives. Only in the present can we be an instrument of change as faithful messengers.

Are you pliable in God's hands, and do you allow Him to live through you in the present? Are you making the difficult changes you need to make now, or do you keep putting them off? Do you live out Christ's life in the present? Do you look back to the past with anger, or with yearning? Do you look forward to the future with fear and concern disguised as hope? The Kingdom of God is in the present, do you live for Him in the present?

Day 54

*"**Remember the Law of Moses, My servant, which I commanded him in Horeb for all Israel, with the statutes and judgments. Behold, I will send you Elijah the prophet before the coming of the great and dreadful day of the Lord.** And he will turn the hearts of the fathers to the children, and the hearts of the children to their fathers, lest I come and strike the earth with a curse."* (Malachi 4:4-6)

God does not judge without warning. The first thing God does before He judges is to clarify the law – what is permitted and what is forbidden. If we break His laws, He warns again and again and calls for repentance. Only after many warnings when there is no repentance and no change in us, does He judge and punish. Someone once said that when we move away from God He first whispers to us to come back, if we do not listen He speaks loudly, and if we do not listen then, He shouts. Only after we disobey these calls does He punish.

His desire is that we listen to His warnings, and correct the situation before there is a need for judgment and punishment. His will is not to punish us, but that we should return to Him.

Here too God first mentions His laws, *"Remember the Law of Moses, My servant... the statutes and judgments."* He clarified what is right and what is not. Throughout the entire history of Israel, He sent prophets time and again to call us to return to Him, and finally He will shout, He will bring back Elijah the prophet before the great and terrible Day of the Lord. He will send someone who brought down fire from heaven, and who was also taken to heaven to shout at us to repent.

It is written about the Son, *"Who has ascended into heaven, or descended? Who has gathered the wind in His fists? Who has bound the waters in a garment? Who has established all the ends of the earth? What is His name, and what is His Son's name, if you know?"* (Proverbs 30:4) The One who ascended to heaven has come to be among us, and has come near to us to call in a mighty voice, *"Repent, for the kingdom of heaven is at hand!"* (Matthew 3:2)

Likewise, with our lives He also sends prophets before the great and terrible Day of the Lord, to warn and call us to repentance. Sometimes these prophets are people who speak directly to us, sometimes He speaks to us through His two witnesses, the Holy Spirit and the written Word of God, and sometimes God uses other means such as difficulties in our lives. He will try everything to bring us to repentance, so that He will not need to judge us.

The test of how spiritual you are is in how quickly you listen to God: do you need Him to shout in order for you to hear, or do you already hear when He is whispering?

A faithful messenger of God learns to listen to the whisper from God's heart, and does not need Him to shout. In everything and in every situation he asks God, "What are you trying to tell me? What are you trying to teach me?" For our God is a God who speaks, teaches and corrects.

One of the signs of wisdom is the ability to listen. It is important for a wise person to listen and acquire wisdom, while what is important for the unwise is to make his opinion known. A wise man knows how to listen, while the unwise does not even hear shouting.

Do you know how to listen? Do you want to be wise? Learn to listen and then you will be able to hear God's direction and warnings. Ask God to teach you to listen, and to make you a listener.

Day 55

"Remember the Law of Moses, My servant, which I commanded him in Horeb for all Israel, with the statutes and judgments. Behold, I will send you Elijah the prophet before the coming of the great and dreadful day of the Lord. **And he will turn the hearts of the fathers to the children, and the hearts of the children to their fathers, lest I come and strike the earth with a curse."** (Malachi 4:4-6)

Family is the foundation stone of society and state. This is the reason why we see a historic unprecedented attack on the family unit. God created the family to pass along His principals, values and love to the next generation. He created the family as a womb in which the future society is developed. He is the one who called every family by name (Ephesians 3:15), who through Abraham blessed all the families of the earth (Genesis 12:3), and before whom all the families of nations will worship (Psalm 22:27, 96:7).

The family is important to God, and that is why the devil concentrates his efforts on destroying the family. This destruction is done through divorce, changing the definition of a family, breaking down parents' authority, blurring the difference between good and evil, bringing confusion to children's identity, lack of values, violence, and the destruction of "old" standards.

When the family is strong, society and state are strong; when the family is weak, society and state become weak as well.

The Kibbutz system is a good example of a concentrated attempt to change the character of society by changing the character of the family. Children lived with their age group instead of with their parents and were raised by caretakers. Everyone who grew up in a kibbutz knows and understands the difficulties and problems it caused them – some need treatment for these problems all their lives – and the fact is that kibbutz communal society fell apart but for a few exceptions. Every organization or group that separates family members, and requires loving the organization or group more than the family is not of God and they will end in ruin.

These verses speak of a future time when fathers do not give their attention to their children, and when children do not give their attention to their parents. This corresponds very much with what is happening today. While God is interested in strengthening the family unit, the devil's attempts are directed at destroying the family, and we see society around us in an advanced state of decay. When family is destroyed, the whole earth suffers and is under a curse.

God's will for which He sends His messengers is to return the hearts of the fathers to the children and the hearts of the sons to the parents. Every one of us who experienced the New Birth knows that one of the first things that happens to us is that God restores within us the love for our families. As children, he restores love and respect toward our parents, and as parents He helps us love our children in a way that will build them up.

This is the last call in Malachi, the last in the whole Bible – to turn the hearts of the fathers to the sons, and the hearts of the sons to the fathers. A call to reconcile fathers and sons, which also means, reconciling all people to God, the father to His sons. The first call in the Bible from the depths of God's heart was, *"Where are you?"* when He called after Adam had sinned in the garden of Eden and was separated from Him. We hear the call of God's love throughout the Old Covenant in different forms, and we are hearing this again in these scriptures as the last call in the Old Covenant, *"Return to Me, and I will return to you"* (Malachi 3:7).

This is God's answer to all of man's complaints. As we see in the book of Malachi, the moment people move away from God they start to complain. When people complain about God starting with questions such as, 'Where was God during the holocaust? and "Why is my life so difficult?" His answer is always, *"Return to Me, and I will return to you"*.

God the Father calls us as His children to return to Him as individuals and nations. In the last verses of Malachi, He tells us that if the fathers' hearts do not turn to the sons and the sons' hearts to the fathers, then the whole earth and not only the family will be stricken with a curse. Repentance unto God or lack of repentance bears consequences in individuals, families, a nation and the entire world. When the children of Israel were exiled, those people who were right with God suffered as well.

The answer to all our personal problems is "Return to Him". The answer to a nation's problems is "Return to Him". The answer to the problems of the world is "Return to Him". In the process of our returning to God, He is the one who took the first step towards us by becoming one of us. He first drew near to us, so that if we wanted to return to Him the road would not be long. He is already near. God does not want to bring judgment - He wants to bring repentance. Draw near to Him, and He will draw near to you.

Day 56

"Remember the Law of Moses, My servant, which I commanded him in Horeb for all Israel, with the statutes and judgments. Behold, I will send you Elijah the prophet before the coming of the great and dreadful day of the Lord. **And he will turn the hearts of the fathers to the children, and the hearts of the children to their fathers, lest I come and strike the earth with a curse.***"* (Malachi 4:4-6)

The generational gap is not something that many people associate with sin. During Bible times there was no generational gap, or if so, it was very small. Generation after generation, people lived together in the same home. The children respected their parents who lived together with them all of their lives. Grandma and grandpa were present, the children dressed like their parents and they spoke the same language. When they grew up the children continued to live as their parents did. A generation was about 40 years, and change took place over a long time.

In the 20th century during the fifties and the sixties a process began that is still gaining momentum. The motive was rebellion against "old" values, and the gap between the generations started to grow ever larger. It has many characteristics and catalysts. Teenage rebellion, different music, different clothes, a different way of speaking, the collapse of authority inside the family, divorce, sending grandma and grandpa to a seniors' home, sexual "liberty", a blurring of the line between good and evil, and other identifying marks are part of the visible characteristics and results.

Today the difference between the generations is noticeable, emphasized and encouraged. The dress code is different, the language is different, the value system is different, and this process is gaining speed.

We also see this in the Lord's body, churches aim at a certain generation, while other generations are almost absent from them. It is evident also in youngsters who seek only the company of other youngsters, since "grownups do not understand me". We also see this when people are not attending congregations anymore, because the congregation is so much "yesterday", and anyway there is fellowship on Facebook, internet and TV.

This is the situation described in these verses. The hearts of the parents are not turned to the children but to themselves and their own self-gratification, or to the standard of life that they wish to have. The hearts of the children are not turned to the parents but to their own age-group, and the result is that the earth is stricken with a curse – the land is accursed. Violence is escalating, families and societies are falling apart and everyone suffers as a result.

The generational gap is like a wound in society and is not of God. It is interesting that God chose to write about it in the last verse of the Old Covenant. His will is not only to bridge the generational gap, but to heal this wound and cause it to disappear. His will is to restore the parents to the children and the children to the parents. Restoring means, to bring back to the original condition.

God does not desire a society that is split up according to age groups, He does not desire a church that is aimed at only a certain age-group. He desires families and churches (and a society) where parents and children live together. A place where there is no generational gap. A place where the youngsters do not only learn from other youngsters who speak their own language, but where there are parents and grandmas and grandpas that can enrich the next generation from their own experiences. A place where the grown-ups want to give and the youngsters want to receive.

A healthy family is a family where father, mother, children and grandparents live together. I know of several such families, and the emotional and spiritual richness is clearly evident. A healthy church is like that as well since the church is also a family. A healthy church is one that is made up of old people, grown-ups, youngsters, youth and children all mixed together. In this setting the relationships between the generations are healthy. The grown-ups pass on their experience and love to the younger generation, and the youngsters respect the grown-ups and listens to them, desiring to learn from them.

In the ten commandments it is written, *"Honor your father and your mother, as the Lord your God has commanded you, that your days may be long, and that it may be well with you in the land which the Lord your God is giving you."* (Deuteronomy 5:16) Honoring previous generations ensures a longer and better life, and it is not speaking here only of individuals and families, but also of nations and society.

The devil knows this, and for this reason he introduced and expanded the generational gap. He is interested in shortening man's days and making them evil. God's messenger labors to restore the generations to each other.

Parents, do you understand your mission in raising your children in the morals of the Lord? Are you willing to give up your own self-gratification in order to see your children grow up in a home that gives them a better basis for life?

Youngsters, do you honor the previous generations? Do you listen and learn or do you think that the time of these old folk have passed, and that they have nothing to contribute?

Do you as an individual act with the aim to heal the generational gap or are you intensifying it? Do you seek the company of other generations or keep to yours? Is your family more important to you than yourself? Do you work towards a mixed church that would be a real family? This is the work of a messenger of God, bringing people and generations closer to God and to one another.

Summary

Being God's messenger first of all means, entirely belonging to God. Afterwards the process begins whereby God makes us His message, so that our lives and words will convey the burden that God gave us, and have sent us out to declare. God has been carrying this burden since the creation of the world, the burden of His love to men that do not return His love. God is faithful in His love and does not stop loving even when the object of His love, mankind, does not return His love, rejects Him, curses Him and ignores Him. In His great love He keeps sending messengers to mankind to try and help us to hear and see His love, but even so we have rejected and scorned them. God sent His Son, Jesus the Messiah, as the strongest and clearest call of love to show us in the clearest possible way what love is.

This is the burden that God shares with the ones who love Him and desire to be His messengers. Those of us who believe in Jesus the Messiah, and belong to Him were sent to be His last and final call before the coming judgment.

Those who belong to Him are transformed into His image and also love people, even when people reject us and refuse to hear the message that God gave us, *"Return to Me, and I will return to you."* (Malachi 3:7). God's messenger is himself the message. He keeps returning to God throughout his life, and demonstrates how God returns to him.

We are to preach His love with words and deeds, become transformed to His image, and find others who will continue to relay the message of God's love.

The apostle Paul, one of God's messengers who carried the message in the clearest way said, *"Imitate me, just as I also imitate Christ."* (1 Corinthians 11:1). To Timothy Paul says, *"And the things that you have heard from me among many witnesses, commit these to faithful men who will be able to teach others also."* (2 Timothy 2:2). Paul passed on the message to Timothy and instructed him to also pass it along to others, who in turn will then pass it further on through the testimony of their lives and in their teaching.

Paul also talks about, *"forgetting those things which are behind and reaching forward to those things which are ahead."* (Philippians 3:13). We are in the process by which we must leave behind the things that were, and change into what will be. Someone wise once said, "Today you become the person you will be tomorrow." My decisions and the things I do today determine what kind of person I will be tomorrow.

John the Baptist understood his place as a messenger of God and said in John 3:30, *"He must increase, but I must decrease."* This is the way he lived his life. This is how we should live our lives as well.

Jesus gave us a commandment and in order to fulfill it we must go out to Him outside the city. *"Therefore*

Jesus also, that He might sanctify the people with His own blood, suffered outside the gate. Therefore let us go forth to Him, outside the camp, bearing His reproach. For here we have no continuing city, but we seek the one to come" (Hebrews 13:12-14)

The question we need to ask God and ourselves is not, "Have I been called to be a messenger?" – we are all called to be God's messengers. Rather ask, "What kind of messenger am I?" In order to get a true answer, we must be willing to look into God's Word, allow God's Spirit to test the depths of our hearts and to shine upon the darkest places inside of us.

In John 7:18 Jesus said, *"He who speaks from himself seeks his own glory; but He who seeks the glory of the One who sent Him is true, and no unrighteousness is in Him"*

Each one's prayer should be, "God, help me to be a faithful messenger in all of my ways, every day and every moment."

My prayer for you is that you will partner with God to carry His burden, and that your life will be a very clear declaration of *The burden of the word of the Lord to Israel by Malachi (my Messenger). "I have loved you," says the Lord.* (Malachi 1:1-2)

And Jesus came and spoke to them, saying, "All authority has been given to Me in heaven and on earth. Go therefore and make disciples of all the nations, baptizing them in the name of the Father and of the Son and of the Holy Spirit, teaching them to observe all things that I have commanded you; and lo, I am with you always, even to the end of the age." Amen. (Matthew 28:18-20)

Therefore, go as true messengers of God to make disciples, who will in turn make other disciples.

Made in the USA
Columbia, SC
17 August 2017